WHEN YOU PRAY

WHEN YOU PRAY

HAROLD LINDSELL

BAKER BOOK HOUSE
Grand Rapids, Michigan

Sixth printing, March 1978

PHOTOLITHOPRINTED BY CUSHING - MALLOY, INC.
ANN ARBOR, MICHIGAN, UNITED STATES OF AMERICA
1978

CONTENTS

I

AN INTRODUCTION TO PRAYER

Most Christians regard prayer as real. But it needs to be rescued from neglect and irrelevance and to be used as God intended. Even beyond the borders of the Christian Church there are multiplied millions of men of other faiths who believe in the reality of prayer, however diverse their understanding of its true meaning and usage.

At San Francisco, when the United Nations was brought into being, the opening session was commenced with silent prayer. Protestant, Roman Catholic, Orthodox, Jew, Mohammedan, Sikh, Hindu, Buddhist, Shintoist and Confucianist bowed together.

But the reality of prayer has always been challenged by some bold opponents who have consigned prayer to the limbo of the discarded or the outmoded. These attacks on prayer, however, have not always come from agnostic and atheistic sources. Some of its severest critics include men who profess to revere religion but find no place for prayer because they believe that God does not intervene directly in the affairs of men.

They are convinced that this planet is governed by immutable natural laws that can neither be superseded nor broken. Theirs is a closed system of naturalism that allows for no outside interference, human or divine. Naturalism is mechanistic and depends for its orderly operation on the arrangement of the cells. It accepts the notion of the uniformity of nature. No thoroughgoing naturalist can believe in free will, for that would mean that human beings have the power of independent action, and the existence of such a power that can originate events is something no naturalist will admit.

The naturalist is a determinist and as such he must always oppose the notion of miracle and the supernatural.

Now, if the naturalist *is* right, then prayer *is* useless. Prayer presupposes the existence of nature and law, but it also presupposes that purposive order can be introduced into the system from without. This allows for novelty and novelty is miracle. In other words, natural law does not cover all the facts. God is involved. He operates from without the system of natural order and does so purposively. God supersedes natural law and he has ordained that prayer shall be one of the causes that occasions his divine intervention in which he transcends his own natural laws for higher purposes.

The naturalist insists that the dead cannot rise. But God intervened and raised Jesus from the dead. The naturalist says that every effect must arise from a natural cause. But God hears prayer and causes rain to fall when there are no natural causes. Virgins who have not known men do not get pregnant. But Jesus was born of the Virgin Mary precisely because God the Holy Spirit intervened in the natural order, and by a miracle she who was truly a virgin was impregnated. Indeed the substantive quality of prayer that constitutes its uniqueness is the fact that God intervenes in the natural order in response to prayer, and does what would not and could not be done had he not intervened. Prayer is based upon the belief in the supernatural, the miraculous. God does intervene directly in the affairs of men and one of the ways he does so is in answer to prayer.

Because God intervenes in the affairs of men, prayer is not doomed—unless men doom prayer by failing to practice it. But as long as the gates of hell do not prevail against Christ's Church so long will prayer continue, and so long will God's people keep on praying. We who confess Christ and pray because he told us to and taught us how to do so will never be surprised or overwhelmed, even though vast numbers of people deny the validity and worth of prayer. No matter how many people reject prayer, this will not keep us from the practice of prayer, nor prevent us from its enjoyment, nor take from us its benefits.

Christendom in its largest and most inclusive sense is in disagreement about many essential and non-essential matters. Some disagreements are so great that they divide one group of Christians from another. But in the matter of prayer, all of the communions which in any sense claim to be Christian are in agreement. All of them confess their belief in the necessity and efficacy of prayer. In fact, prayer is a universal phenomenon common to Christian and non-Christian religions. Whatever the god or gods non-Christians worship, they invoke them in prayer. Christians regard non-Christian prayer as counterfeit, but we may remember that the very existence of the counterfeit presupposes the existence of the real.

Belief in prayer is a far cry from effectiveness in prayer. And the assent of men to the values of prayer does not necessarily mean they practice it. The potential of prayer is jeopardized because so few who say they believe in it speak from personal and continued experience in the practice of prayer.

Prayer, because of what it is, differs widely from other aspects of the Christian faith. Baptism, church membership, the celebration of the Lord's Supper, the election of church officials, and the laying on of hands are concrete acts. They can be seen and felt. They are validated by the same sense perceptions that validate other realms of reality. But prayer does not fit so neatly into this scheme of things. The same factors that govern other realities do not apply here. New categories enter the picture. They are of a kind that are not so readily discernible.

Both the unconverted as well as the converted can see and comprehend baptism, church membership and the others. The unconverted, however, know little about prayer and understand it less. But the same problem may exist for the converted too. They have little difficulty appreciating the reality of those facets of church life validated by the external senses. When it comes to prayer, however, they are confused. Its laws of operation seem so complex and the interaction of relationships so intricate that one hesitates to presume that he understands that which has in it the elements of the mysterious.

The praying Christian speaks and witnesses about receiving answers to prayer. Some years ago Mrs. Jonathan Goforth wrote an entire book that had for its theme, "How I Know God Answers Prayer." Puzzling questions enter the minds of thoughtful people at this point, questions that can quickly cause one to sink into a labyrinth of confusion. Were the so-called answers to prayer really answers? Would not the same things have occurred if there had been no prayer? Was there any divine intervention, and if so why do I not perceive it? These and a host of other queries rise to plague even those people who are fervently committed to a belief in prayer and its usefulness.

While we muddle through the problems connected with prayers that have been answered, we are floored by what seems to be unanswered prayer. One mother prays and her son dies in battle. Another mother prays and her son lives. And sons of other mothers do not die even though no one has prayed for them at all. More complicated is the query that comes to the searching heart, "Had I prayed, would this evil that has befallen me not have happened?" Here, as in many of the questions surrounding the mystery of prayer, cause and effect cannot always be seen. When a man listens to a sermon, decides to confess Christ before men and join the church, the movement from cause to effect is outwardly easy to detect. But when a man prays for rain and his neighbor prays for sunshine, serious complications arise! Then the causal relationships are not so perceptible.

The complexity of prayer may explain why so few Christians wrestle with the problems in an effort to arrive at a better understanding. Many Christians pass through life with a warped perspective and have a dwarfed prayer life because they neither understand nor appreciate what they could know if they really wanted to. Mentally convinced of the value of prayer, they still never get beyond the infant stage of development.

Some Christians approach prayer with the idea that it is very simple. They come up with glowing platitudes and unfounded assertions. They appear to know all the answers. It is far easier to help the uninformed person who admits his lack of knowledge than the one who thinks he knows it all. The former is at least teachable; the latter is hard to reach. Those who are convinced that they know all the answers either lack perception or do not see the problems or are remarkably naive. Unfortunately, prayer does not reduce itself to an either-or; it is neither black nor white. Sometimes it is black *and* white—or just plain gray.

When someone asks hard and perhaps unanswerable questions about unanswered prayer a stock reply is the assertion that "all things work together for good." Now it is true that we do believe that all things work together for good. This assertion may silence the questioner, but silence does not solve all the problems. Let us assume that a mother prays for the safety of her son in battle. Instead of surviving the dangers of war he is killed in action. The words "all things work together for good" will by no means satisfy that mother, unless she throttles her intelligence and smothers the questions that spring spontaneously from the heart. Surely, asking legitimate questions cannot be sacrilegious, and who is to say it is always wrong to pose questions even though we believe that "all things work together for good"?

We *should* ask questions and seek for answers. We may well be saying, "Did I lack faith to believe?" "Was there sin in my heart?" "Was my prayer not in accord with the will of God?" "Is this designed to bring me closer to God or to teach me some other lesson?" One writer has stated that the Christians can ask "When?" "Where?" "How long?" and "What?" but he cannot ask "Why?" There is no Biblical basis for such a statement. Why is it wrong to ask "Why?" The reply to the "Why?" may be precisely the therapeutic agent that is needed to quiet the fears, increase knowledge, broaden perception, deepen faith, and improve the life of prayer. The assumption that "all things work together for good" was designed by God to prevent questions is without the support of logic or Scripture. Only after we have exhausted all other lines of inquiry without avail can we fall back on this Scripture, realizing that there are some mysteries for which there are no pat answers.

Having these things in mind, the purpose of this book is to

throw some light upon the dark places of prayer. I would like to share certain insights with those who have a lively concern for this accepted but often neglected aspect of the Christian life. It is not my purpose to write an apologetic for prayer to silence the guns of the skeptics. I commence with the fact of prayer. I will not try to convince the reader that he ought to pray. If he needs that kind of exhortation he should look for it elsewhere. My approach is explanatory, not apologetical; it is didactic, not hortatory. I wish to share something with those who do pray, or with those who do not pray but who would like to. I write for the converted, not for the unconverted.

The subject is vast, and many writers have contributed to it. There is a perennial need to place old truths in new settings and to add to their luster. I hope to throw new light on old facets and to regrind and polish some facets of the gem of prayer so it will gleam more resplendently. The pilgrim who walks through the world that is not his final home needs all the help he can get. God in his wise providence has provided many kinds of help. One of the greatest is his gift of prayer. It is this gift I propose to discuss in the pages that follow.

II

PRESUPPOSITIONS ABOUT PRAYER

For those who do not believe in prayer, no defense will avail; for those who pray, none is necessary. Anyone who wishes to read a defense of prayer will find this a heavily plowed field. Every library has a shelf full of books to prove that man should pray.

Since we are concerned with the practice of prayer one thing is necessary—to acquaint the reader with the presuppositions undergirding all prayer. These are the "givens," i.e., the foundation on which we intend to erect the superstructure.

PRAYER IS ANSWERED

The first and most obvious presupposition is that *God answers prayer*. If he didn't, there would be no need to talk about prayer at all. How and under what conditions God answers prayer is another matter. Moreover, the assumption that God answers prayer does not guarantee the reality of prayer in an individual's life, or the effectiveness of those who pray, or the number of answers to prayer. A mere endorsement of the premise that God answers prayer will not automatically solve the manifold problems confronting Christians.

If God answers prayer then prayer is serious business indeed. In that event it could never have been designed to mock men or to make a fool out of God. The Christian is convinced for a variety of reasons that his confidence in a prayer-answering God is not misplaced. Preeminent among these reasons is his belief that the Scriptures are true. Repeatedly, God, in one fashion or another, says, "Call unto me, and I will answer thee, and shew thee great and mighty things, which thou knowest not" (Jeremiah 33:3). God has thus committed himself to answer prayer and his promise suffices for those who believe him.

The Word of God the Father is reinforced by the testimony of Jesus Christ the Son, who affirmed, "Ask, and it shall be given you; seek, and ye shall find; knock, and it shall be opened unto you: For every one that asketh receiveth; and he that seeketh findeth; and to him that knocketh it shall be opened" (Matthew 7:7,8). In his exposition of these words G. Campbell Morgan says that either (1) Christ was deceived when he said these words, or (2) he deceived us by claiming what is not true, or (3) he said what is true. If asking, seeking, and knocking do not yield identifiable responses, the consequences of which can be corroborated satisfactorily by the laws of evidence, one must conclude that Christ himself was deceived or he claimed what is palpably false. But Christians have affirmed their convictions for 2000 years that Christ was neither deceived nor a deceiver. What he said is true. Indeed the Lord of the Church can be counted on, so that it is no false claim to believe it would be easier for heaven and earth to pass away than for the word of Jesus Christ to fall to the ground (Matthew 24:35).[1]

Experience confirms that God answers prayer. Reasonable men do not resist subjecting the affirmations of God and of Jesus Christ to the test of experience. God himself tells men to put him to the test (Psalm 34:8; Malachi 3:10). It would be ludicrous to affirm belief in the efficacy and practicality of prayer if in fact the history of the Christian Church affords no instances of answered prayer. It is precisely at this point that the weight of evidence demonstrates the affirmations of Scripture. History is replete with innumerable accounts of those who have observed answers to prayer and who have witnessed to the validity of their experiences. Only faithless and foolhardy people would bypass such records or loudly proclaim that tens of thousands of earnest Christians have been mistaken. To sweep away these testimonials could only mean discarding the same kind of prudential evidences by which most of life's other experiences are validated. It would negate all history, deny all rationality, and lead ultimately to chaos.

No one should succumb to the error of viewing prayer as a means of changing the individual and his attitudes rather than changing events, circumstances, and history itself. Certainly "prayer changes me"—my outlook, my orientation, and my attitudes. But prayer also changes those situations and circumstances of life which are distinctly divorced from any change which may take place in the individual who prays. Often prayer changes both the individual and the circumstances; and sometimes either one or the other by itself. However, prayer is not self-hypnosis that causes one to identify the real with the unreal. Nor does it explain away the external, tangible, concrete facts of life. For a person who has prayed for healing and who has all the external, visible evidences of cancer, to say that he does not have cancer is self-deception and is not truly related to prayer or the promise of God to answer prayer.

We commence, then with the assumption that God answers prayer.

PRAYER IS GROUNDED IN GOD

The ground of prayer is the person or being of God. There is a specific reason why prayer is related to the person or being of God, and when men disbelieve, overlook, misunderstand, or underestimate the reason, then the purpose and place of prayer is lost, or at least diluted.

Theologically, the Bible says sin has separated man from God and unredeemed man cannot pray to God because of his sin (Psalm 66:18; Isaiah 59:2). By himself, sinful man cannot scale the wall which shuts him out from God. The wall itself was erected by God to bar men from his presence. This is man's tragic predicament. His estrangement from his Creator renders it impossible for man to talk to him except under circumstances that preserve both the holiness and the justice of God. Nowhere does the Bible lend any credence to the naive notion that God is in some way obligated to answer the prayers of sinful man or that he *does* answer such prayers. Man cannot bring to bear upon God from Scripture or from experience any promise or pressure which forces him either by reason of his character, or his revelation, to answer sinful man's requests. To drop the matter here would be to cut man off from any fruitful contact with his Creator forever, but this is not the end of the matter. God *does* answer prayer. How, then, is it possible for a holy and a just God to hear and help sinful man? Whatever the answer is, this is the basic underlying reality which makes possible any and all prayer or conversation with God.

Prayer *is* grounded in the person of God, at least in the sense that God himself has ordained the only means by which he obligates himself to man concerning prayer. This comes to man through the redemption which is in Jesus Christ. By whatever name one wishes to denominate or describe redemption, it remains the one basis on which man can approach God in conversation. Theologians may call it the atoning work of Christ on Calvary, the merits of Christ the Redeemer, the fruit of the cross, or the work of redemption—but whatever the name, it is the shed blood of Christ on Calvary that makes it possible for God to hear and to answer prayer.

There is no intrinsic merit in any individual, redeemed or unredeemed, which makes prayer feasible. His earnestness, his labors, his sufferings, and his intentions avail him nothing. He cannot get to God by reason of them, nor will God hear him. God answers prayer *only* because Jesus Christ went to Calvary. There the Redeemer by his suffering and agony pierced that middle wall of partition which separated man from God. He entered once into the holy place with blood to atone for sin. Thus it is Christ's atoning death which enables man with "boldness to enter into the holy place" (Hebrews 10:19).

One writer has stressed the truth that God is the Father of believers. This is a greater wonder than that he answers prayer. Indeed it is because he is our Father that prayer becomes possible, for if man could not pray, God would not be his Father.[2] God stands in relation to the redeemed as Father simply because of

Christ's meritorious work on the cross. This brings us full circle to the conclusion that it is the work and the merits of Jesus Christ which constitute the ground of prayer.

PRAYER IS THE CHRISTIAN'S BUSINESS

Prayer is the Christian's business. Luther wrote: "As it is the business of tailors to make clothes and cobblers to mend shoes, so it is the business of Christians to pray." [3] Prayer, then, is not an option with the Christian; it is an obligation. He does not have the right to choose whether or not he will pray. He must pray. To be a Christian without praying is no more possible than to be alive without breathing.

Prayerlessness is sin. Samuel exclaimed: "God forbid that I should sin against the Lord in ceasing to pray for you" (I Sam. 12:23). Hooker, the famous Puritan, said: "Prayer is my chief work, and it is by means of it that I carry on the rest." [4] It would be easier to conceive of a city without electricity, transportation, telephone service, water, and police protection than it would be to conceive of the Church without prayer. Yet the unhappy truth is that many churches have "supper rooms" for eating and drinking, but no "upper rooms" for prayer and waiting on God. [5]

Someone will rightly ask, "Why is prayer so important?" Or, "Why should prayer be the Christian's main business?" The answer is that prayer is God's indispensable means by which the fulfillment of the divine will is made possible. Even though men, Christian or non-Christian, cannot discover or fully demonstrate that the course of history is vitally related to prayer, it still remains true—God has ordained that his plan for the world will not come to pass without prayer.

Since God's plan for the world and the Church presupposes prayer, Christians ought not bypass it or substitute other activities for it. To do so is both a conscious and an unconscious temptation. Slothfulness and indifference cause decay in the prayer life. But so do activities which are good in themselves but which are substituted for the indispensable and the best. Watt points out that the Church has enough organizers. It needs no more of them. What it lacks is "agonizers" and of them there are too few in every age.[6] It is the Christian who agonizes in prayer who is able to set loose the power which moves the world.

PRAYER HAS NO SUBSTITUTE

Prayer is irreplaceable. Nothing can supplant it. Substitutes are immediately available for almost everything else. An artificial leg is a good replacement for an amputated one. A hearing aid is an excellent device for the deaf. Parts of a man's body can be removed without essential damage, and some can be replaced by plastic gadgets. If radio communications break down, the telephone, the telegraph, the airplane, or the automobile can serve in its place. One could even carry the message on foot. A poor substitute is better than none. Not so with prayer, however. It has no replacement; there are no substitutes.

Sometimes believers are led far afield by circumstances which appear to contradict this thesis. Thus some good Christian work may continue to prosper for a time even though fervent prayer for it has apparently ceased. This may be explained in one of several ways. Perhaps some other person, unknown to those who have ceased to pray for it, has taken over the prayer burden. The work continues and is blessed because fervent intercession has continued. A second explanation is that a work may go on and prosper even after prayer for it has ceased, simply because of the momentum generated by the prayers of earlier days. This might be likened to a bank account on which one can draw until the amount which has been saved has been used up. The saver may not be the user; and the user may be helped and blessed by that which he did nothing to accumulate. But the account will be emptied at last. The life of Samson is illustrative of this. His strength continued for a season even after his consecration to God had been abandoned. He used up the reserve of an earlier day. A third reason is the mercy of a patient God who may continue to pour out his blessing after prayer has ceased, so that time may be granted for repentance and renewal.

The problem is further complicated because the immediate results of the failure to pray are not always apparent. The ruptured appendix, resulting from the refusal to submit to surgery for the removal of the inflamed organ, is much more obvious, and the consequences only too clear. Not so with prayer. We talk speciously of what might have happened if we *had* prayed, and of what did happen because we *did not* pray. But the cause and effect relationship is difficult to detect, and easy answers do not always satisfy even regenerate people. A minister may cease to pray, and redouble his efforts in preaching and personal work instead. He may enlarge his promotional program, spend more time in his study, and keep himself employed in other good activities fifteen hours a day. But until he realizes that other activities are no satisfactory substitute for prayer, and that the productive potential of these other phases of his work peters out as prayer diminishes, his efforts are vain.

A Christian businessman may spend most of his waking hours in the hot pursuit of financial success, believing this to be the will of God for his life. He may even acquire a great amount of wealth through his own efforts and without real prayer. This would lead some to conclude that prayer is either not necessary to this apparent success or that it has usefulness only for other areas of life. Since we know that there are men who do not pray, indeed who do not believe in God or prayer, who have enjoyed fantastic financial success, the problem appears insuperable. In a sense, it is; yet there are considerations that carry weight in such a case. Perhaps this man described above might have been more successful and have accomplished much more for the glory of God if he had prayed. Moreover, his failure to pray, although it did not prevent financial success, may well have left him an empty shell, devoid of spiritual grace, and an inner failure. The final judgment on any life cannot be based on one single category but upon the totality of that life, so that the prayerless but otherwise successful politician, author, minister, or businessman ends up a wretched failure. The amazing paradox of such failure manifests itself sometimes in so odd a fashion that such a person does not think of himself as a failure but as a great success. He is perfectly satisfied with what he is and has done, for he has become blinded to true spiritual reality. This awful sterility and empty void, known or unknown to the

person who is thus afflicted, is one of the threatening consequences
of a prayerless life. In the light of all this, there is indeed no
substitute for prayer.

PRAYER INVOLVES MEN, NOT METHODS
AND MACHINERY

"Men are God's method. The Church is looking for better
methods; God is looking for better men." [7] History has demonstrated the truth of this assertion over and over again. Is it not
strange, however, that when prayer diminishes and the fruits of
Christian service begin to decline, men generally do not turn to
prayer; instead they feverishly speed up their activities, mistakenly
thinking that more complex organization, additional machinery, or
novel approaches will make up the lack. They never do. God
delights to use men, not methods and machinery.

Scripture is studded with spectacular illustrations of men whose
success or failure for God turned on their own personal prayer
relationship to him without reference to armies, machinery, methods, or even personal diligence. When Judah was invaded by
Moab, the children of Ammon, and Mount Seir, King Jehoshaphat
had little to work with. His military might was miniscule when
compared with that of the coalition formed against him. In his
desperate dilemma he called for national prayer and fasting and
publicly acknowledged his country's impotence. It was prayer,
without recourse to human devices, human machinery, or armed
might, which provided deliverance (2 Chronicles 20:1–25). God
was so jealous of his own glory that he forbade Judah to do
anything which might lead anyone to conclude that the army or
any human agency was responsible for the divine deliverance
which was actually the direct result of prayer.

It was Hezekiah's prayer, not his army, which brought deliverance to himself and to his people from the hands of Sennacherib
(2 Kings 19:14–35). Humanly speaking, the odds were all against
him. His chances for victory against Assyria were nil. God used a
praying man, not military might. Jerusalem was delivered and
Judah saved, not on the field of battle, but with the importunate
king on his knees on the floor of the house of God. Hezekiah

fought a good fight, to be sure, but with a strange weapon—the prayer of faith. It was Hezekiah in fervent prayer again, not the skill of the physicians with all of their drugs, useful as these things are, which secured for him an additional fifteen years of life when he was on his death bed (2 Kings 20:1–11).

It was Jacob's prayer, not methods, machinery, or the machinations at which he was so skillful, which brought him favor with his brother Esau and enabled him to return to his own land with family and goods secure (Genesis 32:9 ff.). It was God using a man, not a man using human agencies, which enabled Elijah to restore the widow's son from death.

In a more modern era, it was God using men in prayer, not money, methods, and machinery, which made possible the rise of the great Moravian missionary movement, as these people for years maintained twenty-four hour a day unbroken prayer vigils. It was God who used men as they prayed out a hundred new missionaries to China under the China Inland Mission in 1887. It was "Praying Hyde," not methods and machinery, that blessed India, produced revivals, and won spiritual victories over sin and Satan. It was a praying German pastor named Gossner, touched by God's Spirit, who was personally responsible for sending forth one hundred and forty-four missionaries to the ends of the earth. It was at Gossner's open grave that a single sentence from the final eulogy illuminated this vital truth: "He (Gossner) prayed up the walls of a hospital and the hearts of nurses; he prayed mission stations into being and missionaries into faith; he prayed open the hearts of the rich, and gold from the most distant lands."

Adoniram Judson suffered long and prayed hard, and he left behind him these imperishable words: "I was never deeply interested in any project, I never prayed sincerely and earnestly for anything, but it came at some time—no matter how far distant the day—somehow, in some shape, probably the last I should have devised—it came."

There are thousands of illustrations of God's use of men rather than his use of methods, devices, and machinery. Even redeemed men prefer to search out gimmicks, devise Madison Avenue advertising techniques, or employ research teams and turn to social engineering. But God appears curiously indifferent to all of these things. His ways are not our ways; his thoughts are not our thoughts. In his sovereign operations in the world God watches for men, obedient men, through whom to accomplish his will. Neither organization, methods, or machinery are substitutes for such men, trained in the school of prayer.

PRAYER PRECEDES PREACHING

One common misconception must be corrected among Christians who wish to get the most out of prayer. It involves the relationship between preaching and prayer. In Protestantism, the pulpit traditionally has been central in the work of the ministry and the worship of the congregation. Clergymen have lived through the week for the supreme purpose of preaching on the Lord's Day. Preaching has always enjoyed a unique primacy. But such an attitude is hardly biblical. Bounds analyzed the situation correctly when he wrote: "Talking to men is a great thing, but talking to God for men is greater still. He will never talk well and with real success to men for God who has not learned well how to talk to God for men. More than this, prayerless words in the pulpit and out of it are deadening words." [8]

Inevitably, someone will ask whether the claim can be validated that prayer is greater than preaching and precedes it. Evidences to support this claim are abundant. The early church, and particularly the apostles, ran head-on into this problem. Increasing demands on the time of the apostles made it impossible for them to discharge properly what they believed to be their most important duties— prayer and the ministry of the Word of God. Drastic action was needed. The solution lay in the appointment of deacons to whom was assigned the work of serving tables. The apostles then devoted themselves wholly to prayer and the ministry of the Word. Note the order of priority assigned in the Scripture: "prayer and the ministry of the Word" (Acts 6:4). Surely the Spirit of God sovereignly worked out the arrangement. The truth is that any lasting power in preaching is proportionate to the prayer which precedes and follows it.

The importance of preaching should not be denied, nor should anyone suggest that prayer without preaching is the ideal. Both are essential to the divine order of things, but each must assume its right relationship to the other. In this relationship prayer precedes the ministry of the Word. The very best preparation for preaching is prayer. This does not exclude sermon preparation, but the finest homiletical production is powerless without prayer. Unquestionably, the preacher who is filled with the Holy Spirit has unction and power. But infilling comes through prayer. This is why Christ himself commanded his disciples to tarry in Jerusalem until they were endued with power (see Acts 1:13,14; Luke 24:49). The powerful preaching of men like Peter after Pentecost was preceded by importunate and unremitting prayer in the upper room.

Therefore, we must accept as one of our presuppositions the truth that prayer is foundational even to preaching and must precede it.

PRAYER IS ABSOLUTELY NECESSARY

Prayer is a necessity for at least two reasons. The first is that God has ordained the means by which his divine will is accomplished in the world, and prayer is one of them. We can say in a qualified sense that without the prayers of his people God himself can do nothing. Stated in another way, we cannot suppose that God will do for us *without* prayer what he has promised to do for us only *through* prayer. This does not mean that God is powerless, nor does it rob him of any of his divine attributes. It simply acknowledges that God in his eternal purposes has made the prayers of his children essential to the fulfillment of the divine will. In the same sense, God is dependent upon what his people do. He cannot preach the Gospel to the ends of the earth, for he has made this the task of his people. Therefore, if the world is to be evangelized, it must be done by his children. And if the Gospel is to be preached by them, prayer is an integral part of the process.

The second reason prayer is necessary is that God has commanded his people to pray. This is indisputable from the biblical evidences. Paul enjoined men to pray without ceasing (1 Thessalonians 5:17). Peter exhorted us to watch unto prayer (1 Peter 4:7). Jesus commanded, "Watch ye therefore, and pray always"

(Luke 21:36). Jesus has left us the supreme example of his own life and practice. He spent the night in prayer before selecting the twelve disciples. His practice of prayer led his disciples to request that he teach them to pray. Jesus prayed at the tomb of Lazarus; he spent some hours in prayer in Gethsemane's Garden the day before his crucifixion; he prayed several times while hanging on the cross of Calvary. The writer to the Hebrews speaks of Christ "Who in the days of his flesh, when he had offered up prayers and supplications with strong crying and tears unto him that was able to save him from death, and was heard in that he feared" (Hebrews 5:7). The witness of Scripture allows for no doubt; men ought to pray. But one significant question remains unanswered: "Why has God commanded us to do so?" The reply to this question will enable us to understand why it is necessary to pray, and it will afford us light on the meaning of prayer.

God commands us to pray for a number of reasons. First, prayer is the only means by which we can talk to God. God communicates or talks to us through the Bible, the circumstances of life, and the inward persuasion of his Holy Spirit. But we can communicate with him through the single means of prayer. There is no other medium by which men can converse with God.

Also, prayer is God's appointed method for conferring the benefits and blessings we all need, whether spiritual or temporal. There are Christians who look upon prayer as burdensome, dull, and difficult—an unreasonable duty pressed upon them. They regard it as somehow benefiting God, a kind of favor they confer on him. Surely he has no need of creatures to talk to him so that his selfhood may be gratified or his ego inflated. Certainly God never ordained prayer because he needed it or it helped him. Quite the opposite is true: Man is the one who needs prayer and is helped by it. It is a privilege to engage in conversation with one of this world's great leaders. How much more significant it is to speak with the Creator of all things. But prayer is more than a privilege; it is also a delight. Can anyone conceive of a human being in whose presence he would find greater personal pleasure and from whose conversation he would receive greater blessing than that which would come from being in the presence of Almighty God?

Prayer is necessary because its absence is the surest means of cutting oneself off from God, permitting the spiritual life to wither. Prayerlessness produces sterility of spiritual perception, a life without holiness, and a witness without power. Indeed, the richest of life's blessings cannot be secured save by prayer, as Christ himself taught (Mark 9:29). It is essential to the cultivation and development of the spiritual life. The man who is truly interested in his own welfare must be interested in prayer.

We see then that prayer is necessary, not for the sake of God, but for the benefit and the help of the people of God, who could not exist without it.

PRAYER IS POWER

Christians pray because they believe that God answers prayer and through it his power is released, changing men and circumstances. Having said this, one faces an unresolved problem of the skeptic. Can it be established positively that so-called "answers" were really the result of prayer? Immediately it must be acknowledged that God's method of working in answer to prayer is often concealed so that when scientific evidences are demanded they cannot be produced in such a fashion that they will satisfy the eye that is veiled by unbelief. A given set of circumstances viewed through the eye of faith assures the individual that God has answered his prayer. But when these circumstances are viewed by the eye of unbelief, it sees in them no corroborating evidences. If God does not answer prayer and if men and circumstances are not changed, then prayer does not fulfill the functions attributed to it in Scripture, and it becomes meaningless motion based upon false assumptions. Fortunately for the Christian, innumerable historical testimonies validate the claim that prayer *is* answered and that believers can have confidence in its efficacy.

One cannot dismiss the claims of answered prayers by attaching the label of *fairy tales* to them, for to do so would be to discredit everything in sense experience. Asa cried out, "We rest on thee and in thy name we go" (2 Chronicles 14:11), and he triumphed over the enemy. Hezekiah prayed "We have no might . . . neither know we what to do: but our eyes are upon thee" (2 Chronicles

20:12), and he won a great victory without losing a single soldier. Daniel "kneeled upon his knees three times a day, and prayed, and gave thanks before his God" (Daniel 6:10), and he landed in the lions' den because of this faithfulness in prayer. But Daniel was delivered and he testified, "My God hath sent his angel, and hath shut the lions' mouths" (Daniel 6:22).

In the Thirty Years' War, Gustavus Adolphus' army knelt to pray, and sang "A Mighty Fortress Is Our God," and went on to win a strategic battle. Mary, Queen of Scots, acknowledged that she feared the prayers of John Knox more than any army of ten thousand men. The apostles prayed for ten days before Pentecost, and out of that baptism of power at Pentecost came the movement which shook the world. George Müller prayed and thousands of orphans were fed and clothed. J. Hudson Taylor saw his mission force grow, through prayer, to more than a thousand during his own lifetime.

Of course, it is true that not all who prayed and believed were delivered, except as deliverance came through the merciful release of death. Some were "stoned," "sawn asunder," had "trial of cruel mockings and scourgings," "being destitute, afflicted, tormented" (Hebrews 11:36–38). In them God was glorified by their sufferings, and their prayers were answered even in denial.

Who is able to gauge the incalculable power of prayer which operates in a preventive manner? Who knows what tragedies have been averted because men prayed? Who knows how many lives have been spared through intercession? And who can estimate the evil consequences which have come because no one prayed? No one can validate these aspects of prayer empirically, but they should not be overlooked when we stress the power of prayer and confidently affirm that one of the basic presuppositions upon which we build is that prayer *is* power.

PRAYER IS WORK

The average Christian fails to understand that prayer is work. He tends to envy men whose lives indicate they have mastered the art of prayer, not perceiving that these men attained great heights in prayer because they paid a heavy price. He takes no note that this excellence has come because of the rigorous discipline they have undergone in long, hard days of agony, blood, sweat, and tears. He does not realize that they are men who disdained shoddiness in prayer. Nor does he sense that they mastered prayer because they first mastered themselves. They had a vision of what prayer consists in and they were willing to pay the necessary price to attain excellence in its use.

Prayer in its best and fullest sense is work. It demands of men all that they are and have. This is true for two reasons. The first is that any worthy relationship of redeemed but finite men to God can be maintained only by great diligence. The best spiritual attainments have the highest price tags attached to them. Since prayer offers the maximum in human spiritual development and makes God's mighty power available to the simplest saint, he has chosen to surround and safeguard it by the strictest security. The sacred heights which keep slackers defeated may best be scaled, the precincts invaded, and the power unleashed by those who have graduated from God's school of prayer. The man who cannot discipline himself to rise early in the morning to talk with God is not likely to triumph over his foes or pray through for victory over the adverse circumstances of life. The man discouraged by delayed answers to prayer, will not persevere. There are barriers which must be surmounted; there are lessons which must be learned; there are laws which must be mastered; there are long hours of preparation and practice which must be endured.

The second reason why prayer calls for self-emptying effort is that the opposition of Satan must be overcome if the Christian is to secure a breakthrough. Satan's ministry of disruption is to discourage, defeat, destroy, and disillusion. He has his own great power which he uses to negate the power of prayer. Satan's purpose is to thwart the Christian who prays. "For we wrestle not against flesh and blood, but against principalities, against powers, against the rulers of the darkness of this world, against spiritual wickedness in high places" (Ephesians 6:12). Even as Christ had to suffer death on Calvary before he rose again, so the Christian in his struggle with the Devil must wage a warfare unto blood. Prayer is labor, and demands tremendous effort as well as the deepest commitment on the part of the believer if he is to succeed in the battle against the forces of evil.

Christ found it necessary to spend entire nights in prayer, although he was the Son of God. Likewise, his people must expect to be called upon to spend and be spent. If Christ offered up prayers "with strong crying and tears" (Hebrews 5:7), and if Paul prayed without ceasing, can the tearless, fearful, vacuous, fitful prayers of careless Christians bring forth an abundant harvest? One writer remarks: "When his wife remonstrated with him for rising at midnight to pray, Welsh of Ayr said, 'I have thousands in my parish, and I know not how it is with many of them.' A president of a college, when told that he had but half an hour to live, replied, 'Then take me out of bed, and put me on my knees, and let me spend it calling on God for the salvation of the world'; and he died upon his knees." [9]

Prayer is work. No one has ever succeeded in reaching prayer heights who has not labored and travailed, for such heights cannot otherwise be attained.

PRAYER IS GOVERNED BY LAWS

Man lives in a world controlled and governed by laws. The knowledge and right use of these laws are indispensable to a fruitful and satisfactory life. No one can disregard the physical laws which govern him, without paying a price, sometimes a very high one.

Man lives by breathing. When man ceases to breathe he ceases to live. Therefore, a man cannot remain under water for any length of time without dying. However, fish live *in* water and die when taken *out* of it. Both men and fish survive when they respect the proper physical law of survival which governs them. In the case of man, he can supersede the one law by the use of another law and still survive under water. He can do this, for example, by going under water equipped with an oxygen tank or in a submarine, both of which will permit him to remain there for longer periods of time, but still not indefinitely. A man can hold his breath under water and as long as he is able to do this he will not drown, but again the length of time is limited and the physical law of oxygen and water overtakes him at last.

What is true in the physical realm is equally true in the spiritual realm. Prayer is a spiritual phenomenon; as such, spiritual laws govern it. Just as man's physical life requires the knowledge and use of the physical laws, so man's spiritual life requires the knowledge and use of spiritual laws. The discovery and use of the spiritual laws that govern prayer are essential to the growth and development of every praying person. Prayer, like other areas of life, is governed by its own laws which are peculiar to it. This concept is one of the foundations on which prayer rests.

PRAYER MUST BE LEARNED

Prayer does not come naturally to men. It must be learned. It is not a mere instinctive reflex, although it may exist within man as an impulse. That man possesses an impulse to pray may be demonstrated from the fact that all religions accept prayer as a "given" and all men, sooner or later, and under varying circumstances, engage in what might, non-technically, be called prayer. But prayer as it is understood and taught in the Scriptures is more than an impulse; it is learned following conversion.

Certain physical responses commonly accompany physical life. One of them is breathing, which comes naturally so that infants do not need to be taught to breathe or how to breathe. Swallowing is another physical phenomenon which is an instinctive reflex. One's ability to do these things is not substantially improved by practice or by analysis. They may be somewhat modified, perhaps, but there is little room for change or growth. But with prayer it is different. Unlike physical reflexes, it must be learned, and its effectiveness depends on how well we get our lessons.

Those master prayer best who are acquainted with the theory and the practice of prayer. Perhaps that is why his disciples said to Jesus, "Lord, teach us *to* pray," rather than "Lord, teach us *how* to pray." The petition the disciples put to Jesus included both theory and practice and is thus comprehensive, whereas a request to learn *how* to pray is incomplete. Learning to pray, therefore, includes knowledge of the laws governing prayer as well as experience gained in the practice of prayer. Prayer must be nourished and cultivated if it is to grow.

Learning to pray means that one must be taught, and this assumes both a teacher and a pupil, for the one cannot exist without the other. It implies a learning process. It follows then that the learner advances from the simple to the complex. He makes progress, just as in mathematics one must learn simple arithmetic before going on to algebra, geometry, or calculus. Learning to pray cannot be accomplished in one easy lesson. Mastery of its simplest elements requires patience and practice. Two people can play the same piece on the piano by striking the same notes, but this does not necessarily demonstrate an equal degree of mastery. The notes are the same but the results vary—and this is true in praying. Teaching also supposes that there is something to be taught—to be communicated. Moreover, it takes for granted the idea that the student will place himself in a learning situation, exhibiting the desire to learn and the willingness to submit to the teacher. After that, he who is taught must practice or put into operation what he has learned.

Buttrick takes seriously the admonition of William James on the formation of good habits. "James proposes," he says, "four rules which we might summarize as follows: *first,* the habit should be started with full self-commitment and with a 'burning of bridges'; *second,* the new action or thought should be repeated frequently, and if possible without lapse, especially in the early stages; *third,* the impulse to obey it should be honored without delay, even though the impulse occurs 'out of hours'; and, *fourth,* the habit should be practiced beyond routine regularity and at some cost." [10]

Learning to pray is both taught and caught, but each Christian starts as a beginner and must climb the steep ascent to success; prayer is not an automatic reflex but an acquired skill.

PRAYER HAS MECHANICS

The mechanics of prayer should never be allowed to usurp the place of prayer itself. This does not eliminate a consideration of mechanics, nor does it mean there are no mechanics connected with prayer. The mechanics, however, should be thought of as aids to prayer, not ends in themselves. The great danger always facing any Christian is that of substituting the form for the fact, the external act for the internal spirit, the counterfeit for the real. In Old Testament time the law degenerated into a spiritless legalism, the temple sacrifices lost their true significance, and even prayer became formal and lifeless. In modern church life the forms of worship sometimes supplant worship itself, and the forms become ends in themselves. However, the abolition of forms does not guarantee a return to true worship, since the real problem does not lie in the forms but in the meaning attached to them. In prayer this is also true.

A Christian should have a familiar place of prayer, an accustomed retreat to which to retire in peace and quiet. He should have a regular time for prayer, fixed according to his own circumstances. These are habits, and men need habits, provided they do not usurp prayer so as to make it lose its force and meaning. The Christian must assume some position in prayer. In days past some have knelt, some have lain prone upon their faces, some have crouched, some have stood erect with eyes facing the heavens. The publican stood with lowered face as he beat upon his breast. Whatever the place and the position, the development of habits is helpful.

No one can prescribe the form prayer should take when communion with God begins. Some have cried aloud as they prayed. Others have remained outwardly silent while inwardly vocal. Some have used prayer lists and others have depended upon memory. Silent praying may easily degenerate into a lazy wandering of the mind. Praying aloud may become a device to impress someone or simply an affectation to one who enjoys hearing the sound of his own voice. Kneeling may enable one to lay false claim to piety. But the cure for the abuse is not disuse. The mechanics of prayer do not make prayer good or bad, but are aids when properly used.

Each one must develop and use for himself whatever mechanics will best enable him to pray truly and effectively. Consequently it may be affirmed that effective prayer involves necessary and helpful mechanics.

PRAYER REQUIRES VARIETIES OF PETITIONS

God sets no limitations on the matters men may pray about. Nothing is so small as to be beneath the concern of our Father in heaven. Nothing is too great for him to consider. Prayer changes the individual; prayer changes others; and prayer changes circumstances. It makes no difference whether the need is spiritual, physical, intellectual, or material. The Scriptures abound with varieties of prayer. Some people prayed for healing, some for victory over armed enemies, some for spiritual help, some for the working of miracles. Some have prayed for food, some for the knowledge of the will of God, some for enduement with power, some for hope, some for perseverance, some for sanctification, and some for unity. All who prayed were answered. Some received what they asked for and more; others were denied their requests. All things worked together for good—lessons were learned, progress was made, God became nearer, and questionings were answered.

All the events and circumstances in the life of each believer are of interest to God. Each one can come to him with the assurance that he will not be turned away; that God is interested in the smallest detail of life; that the Christian need not fear to present anything and everything to his Father. Assuming all other things to be equal, he will be heard of God and he will receive an answer. Life's most wonderful privilege is conversation with God. This is the Christian's birthright, along with the promise that God hears and answers prayer.

Notes

[1] G. Campbell Morgan, *The Practice of Prayer* (New York: 1906), pp. 23–25.

[2] Samuel Chadwick, *The Path of Prayer* (New York: 1931), p. 62.

[3] W. H. A. Pritchard, *Real Prayer Explained* (London: n.d.), p. 9.

[4] Gordon B. Watt, *Effectual Fervent Prayer* (Los Angeles: 1927), p. 66.

[5] William Evans, *Why Pray?* (Philadelphia: 1937), pp. 21, 22.

[6] Watt, *op. cit.*, pp. 35, 36.

[7] E. M. Bounds, *Power Through Prayer* (London: n.d.), p. 9.

[8] *Ibid.*, p. 33.

[9] Watt, *op. cit.*, p. 38.

[10] George Buttrick, *Prayer* (New York: 1942), p. 139.

III

KINDS OF PRAYER

"Pray unceasingly" is the command of the Apostle Paul. And when we read that, it sounds simple enough—until we begin. Then suddenly we are faced with the questions, "What shall I say? How do I start?" Certainly Paul was no beginner in the school of prayer. His own prayers show he knew a great deal about the subject and was expert in its practice. But this short imperative, this staccato injunction, leaves us breathless. How must it have sounded to the Thessalonians—unless they had been instructed about prayer and read Paul's command against a background of greater knowledge?

The first thing to remember is that prayer is designed to rescue us in trouble. When in need, pray. If God is God and has power, then that power should be used on our behalf—if God is good and if he is concerned. But we don't need anyone to tell us this. Everybody knows that a man in trouble will cry to a higher power, just as a drowning man will clutch at a straw. Wasn't it said in World War II, "There are no atheists in foxholes"?

It is true, of course, that prayer is designed to help people. We are expected to pray so that we may get things from God; but if prayer is limited to that, there is no need for further talk. However, there is far more to prayer than getting things from God; therefore, it is necessary to ask questions: What kinds of prayer are there? Is there any order of priority in their usage? What is the relationship of each to the other and of all of them to the Christian life?

There are five kinds of prayer.

ADORATION

Adoration is the first and the highest form of prayer. In its simplest and finest form it is the worship and praise of God by one of his children. It consists in acknowledging God as God, in paying to him the devotion of heart he requires of true worshippers, in the creaturely bending of knee and bowing of heart before the creator. Adoration brings one into the truest of all reality for in it he confronts God. In this form of prayer man is truly what God intended him to be, and God is truly what man ought to know him to be. Adoration transcends language, although language may be used, and it appeals to the spiritual and the aesthetic elements of man.

Adoration goes far beyond the province of asking anything for oneself or for others. Indeed, it is gloriously unconcerned about this, and seeks only to stand in the dazzling presence of him who is eternal light, the one who is disclosed only to the eye of faith and through the person of Jesus Christ.

In adoration no promises are claimed; no long lists of answered prayers are recited; no proof is needed to reveal the power of God to hear and to answer prayer; no snares are attached to its practice. It has its own efficacious completeness, so that if adoration alone is engaged in, the aspiring soul needs nothing more. It has already found God. That is enough.

Adoration excludes the agonies of seeking to discern the will of God. Importunity is superfluous. There is a lofty unconcern about "yes" and "no" with respect to petition. It has nothing which might produce anxiety or fretfulness of spirit. It has no corrosive effects and never leads into byways of perplexity or uncertainty. The only temptation attached to its practice is to neglect doing it.

Adoration should be the first prayer uttered by devout lips except, perhaps, in moments of great crisis when ejaculatory petitions, spoken or unspoken, leap from the heart to God for want of time to begin with adoration. When one can engage in serious prayer, in organized and regulated fashion, the place to commence is with adoration. This highest worship of Almighty God consists in being wholly taken up with him, as heart and mind and soul are aflame with the love of God. It is the most intimate form of communion in which the creature adores his Creator, the finite before the infinite, the powerless before the powerful, the nothing before the All. It is not only objective, rational, and of the mind; it is the subjective experience of a mortal man coming in awe with covered face into the presence of immortal Light before whom nothing defiled or impure can abide or endure. Ideally, it is a spiritual experience during which life's temporal realities fade, and competing thoughts and fancies are burned to ashes in the consuming presence of the Lord God. It is the *summum bonum* of spiritual reality.

Jesus taught his disciples that adoration is man's first duty toward God. He commanded his disciples to say, "Our Father, which art in heaven, Hallowed be thy name" (Luke 11:2). God is our Father. Although earth is his footstool, his dwelling place is heaven, where he is above and beyond man in his divine transcendence. The Scripture further affirms that the heaven of heavens cannot contain him (I Kings 8:27). This God who is transcendent is as far off as infiniteness is removed from finiteness and as time from eternity. But he is also imminent and not far from us. He is closer than hands or breathing. We are to hallow, or worship, or adore this God who is both near and far. We are to begin our prayers with adoration. This is the divine priority.

Paul constantly used adoration in his prayer life. Thus he could write, "Now unto the King eternal, immortal, invisible, the only wise God, be honor and glory for ever and ever. Amen" (I Tim. 1:17). That is why he penned the apostolic benediction, "Now unto him that is able to keep you from falling, and to present you faultless before the presence of his glory with exceeding joy, To the only wise God our Saviour, be glory and majesty, dominion and power, both now and ever. Amen" (Jude 24,25). Paul's eye was fixed on the majesty, glory, and power of God. From the moment he was blinded by the light from heaven on the Damascus road to the approaching hour of death, there was no diminution of this conviction. Indeed, his second letter to Timothy closes with this concern to adore God as he says, ". . . to whom be glory for ever and ever. Amen" (II Tim. 4:18).

Hezekiah, in the Old Testament, faced with the pressing problem of imminent invasion by the enemy, first engaged in the worship and adoration of his God. He prayed, saying: "O Lord God of Israel, which dwellest between the cherubims, thou art the God, even thou alone, of all the kingdoms of the earth; thou hast made heaven and earth" (II Kings 19:15). Here Hezekiah acknowledges the sovereign greatness of his God. He adores him as the Creator of the heaven and the earth and as the one who rules over all the kingdoms of this world, even the kingdoms which do not confess his lordship. Particularly, Hezekiah has in mind the fact that God controls Sennacherib and his nation, Assyria, and does with them as he wishes according to his own design and good pleasure.

Jehoshaphat, like Hezekiah, sought the face of God for deliverance. Yet before he uttered his petition for help against Moab and Ammon he paused to adore and worship saying, "O Lord God of our fathers, art not thou God in heaven? and rulest not thou over all the kingdoms of the heathen? and in thine hand is there not power and might, so that none is able to withstand thee?" (II Chron. 20:6). Curiously enough, the words of adoration of Jehoshaphat are not markedly different from those of Hezekiah. Both believe in one God who controls the actions and the destinies of all nations. Both are persuaded that the decisions of the enemies of God's people are controlled by God himself. Indeed, there is a paradox and unfathomable mystery implicit in this conviction. The nations make decisions which please themselves, and thus their right to choose and the resulting responsibility for their choices are not abrogated. Yet at the same time God gets his will done without suspending either his own sovereignty or the power of contrary choice and the consequent personal responsibility of those who exercise this choice.

Even "the heavens declare the glory of God" (Ps. 19:1). The Psalmist asserts that inanimate objects bear witness in symbolic adoration of Almighty God. But behind the cry of the Psalmist, who alludes to nature, is the heart of the Psalmist which bears its own testimony of adoration to God. The voice of the Psalmist may be heard repeatedly in a paean of praise. "O Lord our Lord, how excellent is thy name in all the earth! who hast set thy glory above the heavens" (Ps. 8:1). "Give unto the Lord, O ye mighty, give unto the Lord glory and strength. Give unto the Lord the glory due unto his name; worship the Lord in the beauty of holiness" (Ps. 29:1,2). Nowhere in Scripture is adoration more prominently manifested than in the Psalms. Again and again the Psalmists exultantly and spontaneously break out into exclamations of adoration. "Bless the Lord," "Praise the Lord," "Sing unto the Lord," are parts of their constant refrain. And mixed with both adoration and petition are recurring expressions of trust, faith, and confidence in Almighty God.

The prayer that is preeminently one of petition or even intercession is lopsided, for prayer is not a means simply of obtaining things from God for self or for others. Such a view misreads prayer and drastically reduces its dimensions. To limit the range of prayer to asking for things lends substance to the charge that the one who so prays seeks to manipulate God for his own use.

No Christian can ever use the phrase "my God" as he might use the phrase "my car" or "my house." In the latter instances he does so with the express conviction that these things belong to him and that he has the right to determine what he will do with them even though he may be judged for exercising that right. But when the Christian says, "my God," instead of holding something, he is himself held; instead of governing, he is himself governed; instead of possessing God, he is himself possessed by God. It is precisely in the prayer of adoration that the believer is brought into the proper relationship to God.

Since adoration brings man into immediate and direct contact with God, in the role of servant to Master, of the created to the Creator, it is foundational to all other kinds of prayer. This is not to say, however, that all other prayer is valueless if not preceded by adoration, unless adoration is neither posited nor expressed. The highest ends of prayer are served when begun with adoration.

Analytically, it may be suggested that adoration is composed of worship, reverence, homage, and fellowship. Its privilege and joy consist in dwelling in the divine presence and in being sensitively aware of it. "Be still and know that I am God" intimates that such an awareness is not just theoretical, and that a majestic silence rather than verbose conversation may be a means by which awareness comes. Adoration can be expressed by words or by silent communion, but however expressed, it is heart in communion with heart with no barriers between.

There are snares and difficulties connected with certain kinds of prayer. Not so with adoration. It is an act of self-surrender and emptying in which the child of God finds himself in the arms of God, not grabbing to get things from him but finding in his presence the fulfillment of every unsatisfied spiritual longing and a rest and peace that can be found nowhere else in the universe. It is the story of the restless heart which finds its rest in God.

THANKSGIVING

Thanksgiving is like adoration in that it does not ask things for itself, and unless abused it is not easily subject to misuse. Certainly the most grievous affront and the one most frequently fallen into by those who assert their love of God is simply to overlook the giving of thanks. Thus it is not the misuse of thanksgiving that poses the greatest problem; rather it is the complete omission of it. It is the sin by default, not the sin of offering thanksgiving imperfectly, that so often results in spiritual atrophy and ultimately in impotency.

Thanksgiving is the act of expressing mental or oral gratitude to God for his blessings and mercies. It should be both negative and positive—thanksgiving for those things we have been delivered from or have not had to undergo, as well as for those blessings which we have received. Moreover, the giving of thanks should include heartfelt praise in accepting things we do not like, and thanking God that the apparently evil tidings were not worse ones. Thus it was that John Wesley could thank God that he broke only his arm in an accident and not his head.

Scripture commands men everywhere to offer thanksgiving to God. The Psalmist says: "Offer unto God thanksgiving" (Ps. 50:14). The RSV renders it: "Offer to God a sacrifice of thanksgiving"; the marginal note says, "make thanksgiving your sacrifice to God." The concluding verse of this Psalm is translated, "He who brings thanksgiving as his sacrifice honors me" (Ps. 50:23RSV). In the New Testament Paul enjoins men to give thanks always for all things (Eph. 5:20). In Philippians he advises men to "be careful for nothing; but in everything by prayer and supplication *with thanksgiving* let your requests be made known unto God" (4:6). In Colossians he exhorts his readers to "continue in prayer, and watch in the same with thanksgiving" (4:2). John, in the Revelation, glowingly describes a heavenly scene in which angels say, "Blessing, and glory, and wisdom, and thanksgiving, and honour, and power, and might, be unto our God for ever and ever. Amen" (7:12).

The customary practice of Jesus is instructive in the matter of giving thanks. At the tomb of his friend Lazarus he said, "Father, I thank thee that thou hast heard me" (John 11:41). At the Last Supper he took the bread and the cup and "when he had given thanks" (Mark 14:23), he gave it to the disciples. At the feeding of the four thousand Jesus returned thanks before the food was distributed. In the striking incident involving the healing of the ten lepers the words of Jesus supply us with some pertinent insights. Only one of the ten lepers returned "and fell down on his face at his feet, giving him thanks: and he was a Samaritan" (Luke 17:16). Two conclusions may be inferred from this account. Apparently the nine ungrateful lepers who offered no thanks were Jews and not Samaritans, yet only the Samaritan was sufficiently grateful to return to offer thanks. The second conclusion may be deduced from the biting words of Jesus who said, "Were there not ten cleansed? but where are the nine? There are not found that returned to give glory to God, save this stranger" (Luke 17:17,18). He expected that *all* of the lepers should have been grateful and that *all* of them should have returned after their healing to express appropriate gratitude for what had been done for them. They failed in courtesy, as well as obligation and duty.

If God demands that men give thanks to him, for what shall they give it? Anyone should be able to draw up a long list without exhausting the possibilities. High in order of priority on any list for

the giving of thanks would be the creature comforts we often take
for granted—food, shelter, clothing, a bed, and a home. The
autumn harvest from the good earth, the flowers that bloom in the
spring, the green grass that carpets the meadows and lawns, the
gentle rain that refreshes the parched earth, sun-warmed days and
frosty nights, and nature's thousand other blessings also call for
appropriate paeans from thankful hearts. Multiplied family blessings cry out for appreciation: abounding physical vitality, children
who develop and mature, the altar-bound lassie on her bridal day,
and the scores of incidental but cheer-filled happenings that are
often accepted so casually. Can we not find reason to thank God
for the multiplied blessings of free government, for national peace
and tranquillity, and for those in authority over us? A gospel-
honoring church, a faithful minister, and a concerned Sunday
school teacher may occasion thanksgiving. These and many other
glorious gifts from God should be acknowledged with appreciation,
in the giving of thanks.

Thanksgiving is a normal response as well as an appropriate
one. It is natural that men should react to blessings with thanksgiving. Birds sing. Dogs bark. Trees shed their leaves in the autumn.
They do these things normally and habitually. This is an expression of their innermost nature, a spontaneous outburst that gives
color and dignity to existence. The giving of thanks by men is not
an abnormal phenomenon. It is the absence of thanksgiving that is
abnormal. Just as a cheerful whistle, a happy song, or a radiant
smile reflect the joy of being alive or highlight a human response to
an eventful moment, so thanksgiving expresses the gratitude of a
heart that has been bountifully blessed by a multitude of good and
useful gifts from the hand and heart of a kind and loving heavenly
Father.

Of course, thanksgiving can be abused. A hypocritical spirit is a
canker that festers, a boil that erupts. A classic biblical illustration
of the misuse of thanksgiving appears in the parable of the Pharisee and the publican. Jesus cuts through the layers of pretense
when he says that the Pharisee "prayed thus with himself" (Luke
18:11). The Pharisee deluded himself into thinking he was praying. Jesus says that he was not. When the Pharisee expressed

verbally what was in his heart, he said, "I thank thee, that I am not as other men are, extortioners, unjust, adulterers, or even as this publican" (Luke 18:11). How true it was that he was not like the publican! But this was neither flattering nor a reason for him to give thanks. Whatever the Pharisee thought of himself as he looked in a mirror, God saw him as a sinner. Instead of giving thanks by odiously comparing himself with the publican, he should have been repentant. Had he really wanted to give thanks he should have given God thanks for *His* goodness. But for the Pharisee to thank God for his own goodness (which he did not possess) was an abomination and merely demonstrated how lacking he was in truth, good sense, and taste. If the failure to give thanks is bad, the wicked misuse of thanksgiving is worse.

Thanksgiving, then, and adoration are two types of prayer all Christians do well to engage in and to practice constantly, for with both of them God is well pleased and he is also glorified.

CONFESSION

The third form of prayer is confession of sin. Such prayer is indispensable to the spiritual life and health of every believer. All Christians occasionally sin and fall short of the glory of God. The saints of God come short of absolute perfection in this life. They fail to do always what they ought to do, and what they do do, they do imperfectly. They need daily cleansing from their sins. Obviously we must confess that the regenerate soul who has been justified still remains a child of God whose standing in grace is not broken even though he may commit sin. However, his communion and walk are adversely affected by his sinful acts and conduct. We must allow for the biblical distinction between justification and sanctification. Justification has to do with one's legal status or standing before God. Sanctification has to do with one's life and walk. The former is objective, external, and forensic. The latter is internal and subjective. The former is a once-for-all judicial act which assures the believer that he is accepted in the beloved by faith in Jesus Christ. It guarantees to the believer his positional holiness before God even when he is not yet intrinsically holy during the time of his earthly pilgrimage. In fact, his positional holiness or complete sanctification does not depend upon his living a wholly virtuous life but upon the Holy Spirit, who through Christ hallows the believer by his own indwelling presence. Sanctification is therefore both a completed and an uncompleted work. Experientially it awaits the end of this earthly pilgrimage, when in the glorious resurrection morning we attain to that life and full holiness which lie beyond the grave. Therefore, believers are never relieved of the necessity of having to confess their sins in this life, however pure and holy their intentions may be, for their acts will be imperfect.

The prayer of confession, like adoration and thanksgiving, does not involve the complex of problems or the difficulties normally inherent in petition and intercession. Confession differs radically from adoration and thanksgiving, on the other hand, in one important element. Intrinsic to this kind of prayer is the request for forgiveness and cleansing from sin. True confession that seeks absolution from guilt will always result in an affirmative response by God. He has obligated himself, indeed sworn in his own integrity, to forgive the sins of those who repent and confess. God neither forgets nor breaks his word, so long as man meets the indispensable terms and conditions which he has laid down. Scripture does not speak idly nor does it intend to deceive us when it says, "If we confess our sins, he is faithful and just to forgive us our sins, and to cleanse us from all unrighteousness" (I John 1:9).

The biblical declaration that the sins of believers are forgiven upon repentance and confession does not mean that the temporal consequences of sin are either automatically or necessarily cancelled. To claim or to imply this would do violence both to Scripture and to human experience. Thus the woman who bears an illegitimate child and the man who fathered it cannot ignore or remove the temporal consequences which flow from bastardy. The alcoholic whose physical person has been wrecked and debilitated by excessive use of intoxicants can obtain forgiveness but he cannot reverse the clock to escape from the physical consequences of his dissipation. God will remove the guilt and the eternal penalty for murder upon repentance and confession, but the murderer may still die on a rope or in a gas chamber, or languish in prison for a lifetime. God does not destroy the nature of reality. It stays with us. The consequences that normally flow out of a man's act, however penitent he becomes, may remain. God then supplies boundless grace that enables a man to endure what cannot be changed, and prayer will help to secure this grace of endurance. There are exceptional occasions when the temporal effects of sin may be remitted by God. In David's deliberate adultery with Bathsheba, such was the case. When David confessed, Nathan told him, "The Lord also hath put away thy sin; thou shalt not die" (II Sam. 12:13). The law required that both the adulterer and adulteress die. This was the temporal punishment for this kind of sin. Here God does not demand the death penalty. Instead the child of bastardy died and evil was raised up in David's house against him. Absalom his son revolted and forced David to flee, and how pitiably David wept on the death of Absalom, conscious, no doubt, that this was the fulfillment of the prophetic word and just temporal punishment for his sexual wickedness.

The prayer of confession always accompanies true repentance. The parable of the Pharisee and the publican, to which we have already made reference, illustrates this beautifully. The Pharisee piously thanked God that he was not like other men. His pompous words bounced off the ceiling of the temple because he was a hypocrite. He uttered no word of confession for himself; he felt no sense of his own sinfulness; he had no desire to ask for forgiveness. But the humble prayer of the publican was a prayer of confession, "God be merciful to me a sinner" (Luke 18:13). His penitence led him to confess his sin openly and he received pardon. The Scripture says, "This man went down to his house justified" (Luke 18:14).

Sometimes there is neither repentance nor confession. Such was the experience of Judas Iscariot who brazenly betrayed the Son of God. Caught up at last in the costly consequences of his heinous act and smitten in heart because of his foul deed, he remained adamantly unresponsive in the one place where guilt and death vied against forgiveness and life. But no word of confession burst from his lips, and despite the agony that gripped him as he hurled down the pieces of silver at the guilty feet of his accomplices and vainly sought to whitewash his twisted conscience, he never brought himself to a place of repentance and confession. In still another haunting story, that of the rich man and Lazarus, the essential character of the careless rich man is dramatically unveiled in his conversation with Abraham. All too clearly the lesson is driven home that one's true character remains unchanged by death. What a man is in his inner being in this life does not change for the better when the spirit is separated from the body. The rich man in the grave continued in his essential character as he had been here on earth. Separated from God, and suffering the pains of torment, still no word of confession crossed his lips. Nor does Jesus suggest the barest possibility of a desire to repent. Buttrick observes that his egoistic concentration on himself was not changed by death: "In life he had had no time for Lazarus' needs; he still can think of Lazarus only as ministering to himself" [1] as he entreats Abraham to send Lazarus to wet his tongue with water to assuage his thirst.

The Bible witnesses graphically not only to those who failed to confess; it also depicts those who repented and confessed and who experienced as a result of this act the realized forgiveness they needed to heal their broken hearts and to bind up their wounded spirits. At Calvary the dying thief "rejoiced to see that fountain in his day." He prayed urgently for Christ to remember him when he came into his kingdom (Luke 23:42), indicating his belief in that kingdom and calling Jesus "Lord." His final words manifest both the penitence of his heart and the confession of his sins. Had he been righteous he would have had no need to pray as he did. Sinful, he poured out his confession; dying, he heard the glad word of assurance, "Today shalt thou be with me in paradise."

The story of the prodigal son reinforces the lesson. Reduced to penury and separated from his father because of his own dereliction, desperately facing a dead-end street along the pathway of life, he determined to go back to his father's house. His decision to walk the homeward trail was unaffected by the possibility of a punitive or hostile reception. It went far beyond expediency and represented no temporizing measure for the mere purpose of advancing his material prospects. Sobered as he was with the overwhelming guilt of his delinquency, he was honest with himself and with his father. He made the one choice that opened the only road to deliverance when he humbly cried out, "Father, I have sinned against heaven, and in thy sight, and am no more worthy to be called thy son" (Luke 15:21). This was his confession of sin. The response of his father was immediate and curative. He freely took him back into his heart and into his home—healed, helped, and transformed.

The prayer of confession, an essential ingredient of a conversion experience, does not stop there. In the instances just cited, the prayers of confession were offered by people who were outside the kingdom of God. Truly, no one can walk in peace with God until tained the forgiveness of sins and were granted citizenship in the kingdom of God. Truly, no one can walk in peace with God until there has been confession. This starts with one's awareness that he is lost and must confess his sin and seek forgiveness if he is to be redeemed. It is also true that God unfailingly pardons and receives sinful men who repent and confess, asking for forgiveness. But what about the person who is already in a state of grace, who has succumbed to temptation and is laden down by a sense of guilt and frustration, knowing that his fellowship with God has been impaired? Does he have no need to pray the prayer of confession? Is there no balm in Gilead for him? Does justification cover all future sins which the believer may commit and thus make further confession unnecessary and a sense of guilt a neurotic rather than a real thing? Every believer is confronted with this problem. All have been wounded by the darts of Satan. The sins of a believer can be hidden neither from himself nor from God. Must the saint of God suffer through this life from an enduring and intolerable sense of guilt even while he is justified? Can he suppress and hide his guilt, pretending that it is non-existent? Shall he seek to wall it off from life like a skeleton tucked away in a dark corner of an unused closet?

There is a form of confession that is spiritually pathological and thus abnormal and unhealthy. It is a disease because it is an aberration. The Christian is abnormal who persists in disinterring the decayed corpses of past sins and who delights to dwell on them in masochistic contemplation and rehearsal. If God really casts our

sins behind his back and remembers them against his children no
more, we should refrain from calling them to mind upon every
occasion. It is possible to gain experience and learn lessons from
former mistakes while at the same time burying the incidents
themselves. There are, however, those who do not forget the
incidents and consequently do not learn the lessons. Nevertheless,
there is greater danger in the failure to confess known sins than in
using confession in a morbid and introspective manner.

True confession is genuinely therapeutic. It produces immediate
blessing and sure release. The knowledge that confessed sins are
forgiven sins is purifying and curative. This, of course, has to do
with the believer's impaired fellowship with God. The barrier
erected by the sin is broken down through confession. The fellowship is restored. There comes a sense of repaired rightness of
relationship, of renewed communion that springs out of confession.
But confession penetrates more deeply than this. It works healing
to the wound incurred in the heart. Just as the surgeon lances a
boil to permit the infection to drain and to heal from the inside, so
confession opens the sore, drains the poison, and heals from
within. Scars will be left, to be sure, but this should be regarded
positively, not negatively. In the negative outlook one draws attention to the scar as though it were a defect, whereas when looked
upon positively the scar is to be seen as evidence that the illness
has been healed. So the scar itself is the sign of health, of former
disease that has been conquered.

Scripture affords no better example of repentance and confession in the experience of the believer than the life of David, whom
we have already mentioned. His case study should not be looked
upon as normative as to the kinds of sin involved. Yet the odious-
ness of his conduct and the grossness of his sins, followed by
forgiveness, supply hope to all who have sinned. Any Christian is
apt to conclude that his own sins are quite unlike those of David in
that they are relatively minor and insignificant. He may think he
can take refuge and comfort in the notion that since they are minor
he has no need to confess and to forsake them. But such is not the
case. A tiny pebble in one's shoe will raise a blister and halt the
march just as surely as a greater injury. A minor dislike may

appear as nothing over against a great hate. A tiny lie may seem grey compared to the big one. Yet all of them, small and great, disrupt fellowship and communion. All of them must be dealt with by confession and cleansing. The small as well as the great yield their own harmful harvest in the daily life if they are not taken care of.

Underlying the prayer of confession is the understanding that it is made to God and not to men. Of course this is true, for it would be unbiblical to believe that confession to a man, however well intentioned and truthful it may be, can in itself solve the problem. David admitted his sins to Nathan, but he confessed them to God and asked his forgiveness. Had he acknowledged his transgressions only to Nathan he would never have been cleansed. There is no need for an intermediary other than Jesus Christ between man and God. But this does not rule out the propriety of confession to God *and* to man when understood in proper perspective. Man is not independent of man. He cannot live to himself. In the providence of God there are times and circumstances when deliverance comes, in part, from the assistance rendered by man to man. If confession is to be made to man as well as to God it must be done by freedom of choice as to the person, and the time, and what shall be revealed, so that the dignity of human personality remains inviolate. In general, secret sins should be confessed secretly to God alone; private sins against a brother should be confessed to the brother; sins of a public nature should be repented of and confessed publicly. Therapeutically the Bible, in the context of the teaching that we are to share one another's burdens, shows that the Christian may help his brother by listening to his confession and providing him with spiritual help and counsel in the solution of his problem even though he cannot provide forgiveness or pronounce absolution.

We cannot forget that the prayer of confession must include not only those sins a believer has committed and which he knows to be wrong; it must also bring to God the sins of omission as well. The pharisaic Christian who huddles protectively over a barrel of gold while his brother starves to death has sinned by failing to supply his brother's need. The believer who watches someone drown without lifting a hand to rescue him has sinned by what he has not done. For "to him that knoweth to do good, and doeth it not, to him it is sin" (Jas. 4:17).

PETITION

The fourth kind of prayer is petition. The term as it is used here needs to be defined more particularly. For our purposes, petition covers those requests made to God by the individual who presents his own needs and concerns to his heavenly Father. He is making requests for himself and is concerned with his own interests. When he asks God for things for others he is engaging in the priestly prayer ministry of intercession, of which more will be said later.

To ask God to supply one's own needs and solve one's own problems is legitimate. Scripture everywhere encourages and commands believers to do just this. In the ministry of Jesus when he faced the sick, the blind, and the maimed, he constantly asked of those who needed his help this question: "What wilt thou that I should do unto thee?" (Mk. 10:51). Jesus never once intimated that it was intrinsically selfish or wrong for men to be concerned about themselves and their legitimate needs. Rather he afforded them every encouragement to ask so that they might be helped.

The Old Testament reflects a similar pattern. David cried out, "*I* sought the Lord, and he heard *me,* and delivered *me* from all *my* fears" (Ps. 34:4). The book of Psalms is replete with the personal petitions of individuals who petitioned God constantly for divine deliverance in the midst of pressing problems. Over and over again the phrase "deliver me," or one like it, may be found in the Word of God. Jeremiah professed to be revealing the mind and expressing the will of God when he wrote words directly attributed to God: "Call unto me, and I will answer thee, and shew thee great and mighty things, which thou knowest not" (Jer. 33:3). Any serious student of Scripture must agree that this was intended to encourage men to seek the aid of God for their own needs. The problems we face with petition do not arise at this level. They emerge, rather, after men have already discovered they are encouraged to ask God for help and begin to do so.

There is an order of priority in the forms of prayer. Adoration,

thanksgiving, and confession precede both petition and intercession. There is also the priority of persons and their interests. God
properly and rightfully belongs in first place; one's neighbor is
second; and oneself is third. Surely God is dishonored when a
believer rushes into his presence demanding a thousand things for
himself with little or no regard for the adoration of God or the
needs of other men. When petition that centers in self-needs
occupies a commanding position and becomes the dominant drive
in any prayer life it is incontrovertible evidence of defeat in that
life. The person who allows petition to become central in his
prayer life has already been overcome by his ego and fallen into
the trap of pride. However grave the problems faced and however
justifiable the stance may appear to be under these circumstances,
such conduct and attitude in prayer cannot be excused. It can,
however, be understood sympathetically and efforts made to deliver the one who has fallen into the trap. Prayer may be conceived
of as a circle made up of five parts, each having its own proper
proportion, as illustrated in the circle below (Fig. 1). When the
petition phase of prayer is distorted by an excess of attention, the
remainder of the prayer life is stunted and dwarfed, as may be seen
from Figure 2. When anyone spends most of his time asking for
self, he has done violence to God, himself, and his prayer life.

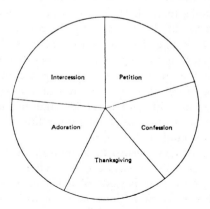

Figure 1

Figure 2

Petition presents other problems that are equally acute. Whereas there are few, if any, snares in adoration, thanksgiving, and confession, there are many snares connected with petition. Indeed, it is at the level of petition and intercession that most of the problems of prayer arise. Inadequate understanding in this area may result in dismaying failure to get positive answers from God in petition, and lead to defeat in the areas of adoration, thanksgiving, confession and intercession. Anyone who is convinced that God does not respond to his petitions is unlikely to engage in the adoration or in the giving of thanks to God. He tends to judge the value and the efficacy of the other kinds of prayer by the results he experiences from petition. He is like the man who concludes that an electric typewriter is useless because it will not work but who does not know or realize that it does not work because the cord is not plugged in. Therefore, it is of the utmost importance for the Christian to grapple with and to understand the problems connected with petition so that his total prayer life does not become warped and his spiritual vitality sapped.

In petition the believer has to face squarely the problem of the will of God. He does not always obtain what he asks for. Sometimes he must endure long periods of delay in which his prayers seem to be unanswered. Sometimes he is amazed to discover that God sends the exact opposite of what he has asked for. Without a proper foundation on which to rest he becomes discouraged and then he ceases to pray. Prayer seems to be a futile exercise. He feels that he is knocking on doors tightly sealed, that he is trying to breach impregnable walls. Finally, he may come to the conclusion that God does not answer because he does not know how to pray. He is not acquainted with, or he fails to lay hold of, the laws which govern prayer. Ignorant of them, or failing to use them, he is impotent. But he does not know *why* he is impotent. Confused and confounded, he falls to the ground defeated and slain.

A believer may know and make use of the laws which govern prayer, but he encounters still other blocks and barriers that baffle him. Perhaps he has unconfessed sin in his life. Perhaps he has asked amiss. Perhaps there is a conflict of interest at the personal level or in connection with prayers offered by other believers. Whatever the problems, the believer may be confused, dismayed, and even defeated. Another section of this book will consider such problems as these and suggestions will be made to resolve them.

Since petition is part of the divine plan for prayer and since God encourages his children to ask, and requires that they expect to receive answers from him, we need to explore the kind of petition they ought to offer. The basic presupposition behind petition is the conviction that nothing in the lives of his people is beyond the concern of God. No matter is too minor and none is too great to stand outside the range of God's sympathetic and listening ear. The death of a loved one is radically different from the loss of a fountain pen. They are self-evidently of unequal importance in any relative scale of values. Yet while they differ relatively, both of them belong within the orbit of God's overarching interest. Just as the child artlessly brings his wants both great and small to his human father, so the child of God ought instinctively to bring all of his wants and wishes to his heavenly Father. Moreover, the relative significance of the death of a loved one and the loss of the fountain pen may vary widely depending upon the individual and his spiritual and psychological orientation. One believer may suffer severe traumatic shock from the loss of a loved one, while another may be but slightly moved by it. The loss of a fountain pen may be of no concern whatever to one individual and of major portent to another. Since petition is inextricably tied to the person who prays, he has no need to be unduly disturbed by what others consider to be important or what they think he should pray for. He must grasp perceptively the principle that God is concerned about *every* detail of his life and then proceed to enjoy the glorious freedom of offering his petitions at all times and for all matters.

Petition

Be not afraid to pray—to pray is right.
    Pray, if thou canst, with hope; but ever pray,
Though hope be weak or sick with long delay;
    Pray in the darkness if there be no light.
Whate'er is good to wish, ask that of heaven,
    Though it be what thou canst not hope to see,
Pray to be perfect, though material leaven
    Forbid the spirit so on earth to be;
But if for any wish thou darest not pray
Then pray to God to cast that wish away.

—Hartley Coleridge

Petition must not be seen as a mechanical device by which the believer forces God to grant him what God does not wish to bestow. Nor is prayer some neat, tricky formula, the use of which will automatically bring health, wealth, and fame. There are drum beaters who declare that God loves to be used by men and the more men use him the better God likes it and the more he can be used. These same people boldly assert that the sick will be made well, the poor will become rich, and the unknown will become famous. Nowhere does the Bible teach that God is the captive of men or that he exists primarily or simply to give them what they want. God is the Creator. Men are his creatures. His own glory comes first. Whoever acknowledges that he is a creature and subordinates himself and his interests to the will of God has a limitless right to petition. It then assumes its proper place in the plan of God and has for its chief emphasis and purpose the glory of God.

Petition underscores man's helplessness and extols the sovereign power of a beneficent God. Petition is not truly petition if it does not operate on the premise that the strongest and most self-sufficient person is always at the end of his tether. If it appears that he has no need of God one way, he surely will need him another. Thus the wealthiest man is no less dependent upon God than the poorest man. The highly educated man is no less dependent than the wholly ignorant or illiterate one. Each is indubitably dependent in a different way and with varying dependencies, but each is dependent. Each needs God. Survival without God is impossible for the unbeliever except for God's common grace. But while the believer may suppose he can go on independently of God, the moment comes inevitably when he is stripped of his sense of adequacy and must throw himself upon God for help. Still the child of God is no destitute beggar who hungrily grabs a few crumbs from the hand of a rich man while he grovels in the dirt and beseeches with outstretched hand. God's children were created in his image. In right relationship to God they enjoy infinite dignity and worth. The true believer comes not as a fawning slave but as a redeemed son whose value must be comprehended as somehow related to the price God paid for his redemption—the propitiatory and substitutionary death of the Son of God on the cross.

Petition belongs unmistakably to the people of God. It is theirs for continued use. They are not to neglect it. It promises the highest rewards. It demands dedication and sacrifice. It searches the hearts of men and reveals what stuff they are made of. The cure for any abuse of it is not its disuse or abandonment. The challenge to develop and to perfect petition is perennial. No one has fully understood its vast potential; no one has exhausted its immeasurable resources; no one has ever been limited in his proper use of it. It beckons all who would employ it and promises the "exceeding abundantly above all" that comes from the heart of a loving Father in heaven.

INTERCESSION

The fifth kind of prayer is intercession. Like petition, it asks God for specific things. Unlike petition, which asks for self, it asks for others. Like petition it is accompanied by many snares. There is the need to discern whether the requests are according to the will of God. Another problem involves entreaties that are denied or delayed. Then there are the reasons why intercession has been ineffective—occasioned by sin in the life, lack of faith, or lack of knowledge.

Intercession has at least one dimension not normally a factor in petition. When one prays for himself and for his own needs other people are excluded. But when one intercedes for another, to his own person there must be added that of the one for whom he is praying. Since the one who intercedes cannot choose for others as he chooses for himself, his prayers for others are complicated by their power to choose. They may be unmoved by prayer or even antagonistic to it. They may battle against the good, or be indifferent to it.

Intercession also tends to be less passionate in its importunity. It is easier to "pray hard" for oneself than to do so for others. The agony of the man who prays for himself and experiences the problems and pains too is always more real for him than the agony and involvements of others for whom he prays but whose experiences are not his own. Thus intercession centers in circumstances different from those of petition and requires another focus if it is to be seen in its true dimensions.

Intercessory prayer eloquently expresses one's solicitude for the well-being of others, whether relatives, friends, or even enemies. Its necessity springs, in part, from the inability of the interceder to meet the needs of those for whom he prays. This is the key to the essence of intercessory prayer. Whoever has the ability to meet the needs of the person he would pray for should do so. The fact that he cannot meet those needs does not relieve him of a legitimate interest in their problems or of his responsibility. "I am my brother's keeper" is not wishful idealism; it is a living reality. Intercession, therefore, supposes one's own inability to meet the need, one's interest in the plight of the person who has the need, and a dependence upon God to meet that need.

The Bible is replete with accounts of men deeply concerned for others and committed to their interests. They threw themselves into intercessory prayer with abandon, not for personal gain but for the help of others. Jesus demonstrated his loving care for friends in many instances. In his high priestly prayer he interceded for his disciples. "I pray . . . that thou shouldest keep them from the evil" (John 17:15); "Sanctify them through thy truth" (John 17:17). Jesus prayed for Peter in a special way. "Simon, Simon, behold, Satan hath desired to have you, that he may sift you as wheat: but I have prayed for thee, that thy faith fail not" (Luke 22:31,32).

Paul, whose life in some measure approximated that of Jesus, ceaselessly interceded for the churches he founded and for the people he shepherded to Christ. He wrote, "We . . . do not cease to pray for you, and to desire that ye might be filled with the knowledge of his will in all wisdom and spiritual understanding" (Col. 1:9). He commanded Timothy: "I exhort therefore, that, first of all, supplications, prayers, intercessions, and giving of thanks be made for all men" (I Tim. 2:1).

The Old Testament depicts noble men who were unselfish intercessors. Abraham leads the list in his impassioned plea for God to spare Sodom and Gomorrah. Over and over again he importuned God on behalf of the righteous within those cities. Indeed, it has been said that God did not leave off answering until Abraham left off asking. He commenced his plea by asking God to save those wicked cities if fifty righteous people could be found within them. He pressed on until God promised that even if there were only ten righteous there he would not destroy them. The tragic aspect of that incident is the dismal fact that there were not even ten righteous people in both of those degraded and profligate communities. The glory of it lies in Abraham's fervent concern as he pleaded for the suspension of divine judgment.

Samuel the prophet spent a night in prayer for Saul. He prayed continually for the people of Israel. King David interceded with God again and again for his people. Moses entreated God not to destroy Israel when he caught them in apostate and gross licentiousness upon his return from the mountain where he had received the ten commandments. So intense was the entreaty of Moses that he prayed, "Yet now, if thou wilt forgive their sin—;

and if not, blot me, I pray thee, out of thy book which thou hast written" (Ex. 32:32). Daniel prayed for the return of Israel to the land from the Babylonian captivity. Joshua interceded for Israel when judgment fell upon them for the sin of Achan. Solomon asked for wisdom that he might rule well over the people of God. Ezra interceded for the remnant in the land that God's wrath might be averted because of the sins of the people.

During the long history of the Christian Church many biographies have been written and many stories recorded of men whose lives were a sweet savor of ceaseless intercession. The Moravians maintained a twenty-four hour a day prayer vigil for lost souls on the harvest fields of the world and for their missionaries working among them. John Knox cried out: "Give me Scotland or I die," so great was his concern for the redemption of his people. Pastor Gossner of Germany was responsible for the sending out of 144 missionaries and it was said of him that he prayed up mission station walls and moved hearts to contribute money so that thousands of the unsaved could come into the kingdom of God. Praying Hyde saw India stirred for God by the power of his prayers. During the dark hours of the night Hudson Taylor was on his knees in vermin-ridden Chinese inns praying for his co-laborers in inland China. George Müller fed and reared thousands of orphans by his intercessory prayers to God. Beyond all of this there has never been a more sublime moment or greater self-denying intercessory commitment than when Jesus in his dying agony prayed for those who had crucified him, saying, "Father, forgive them; for they know not what they do" (Luke 23:34).

In intercession there is a boundless glory that is unhampered by space and time limitations. It is physically impossible for the most compassionate friend to lift his hand to help a missionary instantaneously who is five thousand miles away in some secluded spot in a far-off land. But he can aid that missionary by prayer. Distance is no bar, space no barrier, to reaching the remotest place on earth. Nor is the power of prayer diminished by the distance between the person who prays and the person who is prayed for. It is no more difficult to pray for someone thousands of miles away than it is to pray for a next door neighbor. Intercessory possibilities extend far beyond the people one is personally acquainted with. Through intercessory prayer the believer can touch hearts of Christians he has never seen and reach places he has never been. It is often very beneficial for the person who prays to be far removed from the person for whom he is praying. In this contingency he cannot exert human pressures, voice opinions, or use personality to control matters or determine answers. His only resource is prayer. Men and nations can and do have their destinies decided by God's praying people who through intercessory prayer wield a power greater than the armed might of the nations of the earth.

Intercessory prayer works unseen. Indeed, in most instances, its presence is unfelt and unknown. And even when its work has been fully accomplished, those for whose benefit the prayers have been offered may still have no consciousness that someone had prayed for them. Since prayer must always be related to the person and work of the Holy Spirit, we must mention how the sovereign Holy Spirit works through the unconscious realms of a man's life to bring the will of God to pass. Thus the person prayed for often makes a decision that he believes to be his own, and it is. But it is also a decision effected in his life by the Holy Spirit whose work, in turn, is related to the intercessory prayers of other people. This is true in the lives of both the saved and the unsaved.

In international affairs the Christian should also know that his prayers influence the decisions of unregenerate rulers. Motivated by evil designs and hostile to the Christian faith, such malign characters can and do make decisions they think will benefit their evil ends. The truth is, the very decisions they make of their own choice and in line with the facts they possess work out to produce their own defeat and bring to pass the fulfillment of the will of God. They make their decisions for evil. God uses those decisions for the good of his people and his own glory. And the intercessory prayer is the secondary instrument of God which ultimately produces results in accord with the plan of God for righteousness.

Intercessory prayer, like petition, is the object of satanic attack. The hosts of darkness assault the one who so orders his prayer life. The consequent battle defies description. The warfare is no less real because it is not waged with bombs and bullets. Our opponents are physically invisible; they are not flesh and blood. They are principalities and powers. They are the hidden but powerful forces of wickedness. By deceit and subterfuge these enemies work to vitiate the power of prayer by enticing Christians to spend their energies on other and less useful struggles. One diabolical strategem is to set believers against believers so that they have no time to fight the real enemy. More subtle, but equally potent, is the enticement to ignorance by which the enemy causes believers to misunderstand the true nature of intercession. Somehow they are deluded into supposing that prayer is only a preliminary to their real work, or that it is something which they engage in *after* their main work is completed. This is not true. Intercessory prayer is *the* work. It is tough, hard work. It is taxing labor. It is wrestling before God. However exhausting this wrestling may be, it succeeds because it is grounded in the one principle which assures ultimate victory.

Genuine intercessory prayer is grounded in love. Men adore and worship God because they love him. They confess their sins and ask for forgiveness because they love themselves. They petition God to supply their own needs because they love themselves. But they engage in intercessory prayer because they love others. Love is more than mere concern. Love discerns the needs and problems of others. Love goes beyond sympathy to empathy. Love weeps with the downcast and brokenhearted; it rejoices in their successes and triumphs also. Love sees the plight of men as God sees it. Love reflects the love of God who so loved the world that he gave his Son. Intercessory prayer which is not grounded in love is ineffectual. But when it finds its motivation in love it becomes a powerful instrument for good. From such prayer there flows forth healing, helping, and holy good for a world scarred by sin and desperately in need of a balm.

Prayer consists in adoration, thanksgiving, confession, petition, and intercession. Prayer, to be complete, must include each of these. The continued absence of any one of them means an incomplete prayer life. We are to pray without ceasing, for there is no vital Christian life without it. Each form of prayer must be learned; each has its peculiar function, laws, problems, and satisfactions.

No prayer can be prayed which does not take one or another of these forms. The perfect prayer patterns itself along the lines which have been suggested and the effects which flow from such prayer are great and wonderful. A life without prayer is lived on the margin of the finite, but a life lived with prayer falls within the borders of the infinite. So let the people of God pray that they have power with the one whose power rules the world and whose Word lives and abides for ever.

Notes

[1] Buttrick, *op. cit.*, p. 121.

IV

THE LAWS GOVERNING PRAYER

God created all things, including prayer. All of his creation is governed by laws, the knowledge of which enables man to relate himself properly to the world in which he lives. Because the world is governed by laws it has a predictable orderliness and consequently a dependability. Biblically this is known from God's providence which includes his preservation and government. All things hold together in Jesus Christ, and are held together and will be held together. Christ does this by "natural" laws. The same Christ to whom all authority has been committed in heaven and on earth is the world's governor. He has control over the creation. All of this holds true both in the natural and in the spiritual realms.

In the natural realm man becomes familiar with its laws from earliest childhood. He orders his waking and sleeping by the rising and the setting sun. He does not jump out of tall trees because the laws of motion and gravity cannot be defied. He doesn't put his finger on glowing metal because it would blister it. He sees that two objects cannot occupy the same space at the same time. He observes the movements of the stars and notes that they travel in fixed and predictable paths. He watches birds as they sweep and soar above the earth but he knows that he cannot fly like a bird. He learns that plants grow out of the earth, not rocks or sand. Most of all he quickly perceives that he must accommodate his life to the laws that press in on him if he is to avoid unfavorable consequences and make his physical existence livable. He conforms to these laws; they do not conform to him and he cannot break them with impunity or bend them to his will.

What is true in the physical realm is also true in the spiritual realm—with this difference. The physical realm has to do with things of sight, smell, sound and the outward or visible senses. The spiritual realm includes all of this, but there is an added dimension, one that is more intangible and oftentimes more felt than observed. But it is not less real because it is not always sensible. The awareness of the spiritual dimension depends upon a spiritual sense rather than on the physical senses.

The world of the spirit is governed by spiritual laws just as the physical world is governed by its own laws. There is a major difference, however, in the manner by which the laws of the spiritual order are made known to men. They cannot be discovered by man's search and inquiry through natural and scientific channels except in a cursory and fragmentary fashion. They belong to the order of divine revelation and have been made known to man through the holy Scriptures. These laws are not made by man and he is just as subject to them as to the physical laws, and how he relates himself to them determines his spiritual condition.

God's spiritual laws operate in perfect harmony with each other. One law cannot supplant another one, nor can good or bad intentions nullify any law or invalidate it. Ignorance of spiritual laws and their operations is as devastating in its consequences as the refusal to recognize and obey them. This pivotal truth may be illustrated in the law of salvation. The unconverted individual may be ignorant of the divine law that makes it possible for him to become righteous in the sight of God. In his ignorance he may try earnestly to live a good life and in every way seek to show by his acts that he has a heart of perfection toward his Creator. But according to the spiritual law governing salvation and upon which salvation itself rests, this person is just as surely separated from God as the one who, though acquainted with the law of salvation, openly defies it. To be sure, the enormity of the guilt in these cases will vary greatly, but the standing of each one in the sight of God is unchanged. The law of salvation excludes the possibility of becoming righteous by seeking to live a good life or even by praying. Wonderful as these are and effective as they will be when used properly, no one is justified by them. A man is justified when, in obedience to the law of salvation, he makes a decision by an act of will and confesses Christ as his Redeemer. No other means will avail him anything. There is, then, a spiritual law that governs salvation—the law that for the sinner to be converted he must believe on, and receive, Jesus Christ as his Savior.

A similar truth pertains to the financial life of a church. God has appointed the tithe as the means by which his kingdom is to be properly and adequately supported. A church may substitute suppers, dances, bingo, bridge parties, plays and bazaars. But experience ultimately demonstrates that churches do not thrive either financially or spiritually on this sort of system. Only when God's people bring the tithe of what he has given does the church move forward dynamically. God has promised also that he who obeys the law of the tithe (not conceived of here as a legalistic device but as a voluntary response to the love of God) will be blessed in every way and will not suffer financial loss for his faithfulness (see *e.g.* Malachi 3: 1ff). Whoever makes his gift to God according to the divine method can rest assured that God will make the remainder go as far as the total sum, and see that he does not suffer in comparison to those who refuse to obey the commandments of God. But even if the gift of the tithe were to impair the Christian's income there are other blessings that far outweigh the sacrifice. Moreover, God is especially pleased with gifts that represent genuine sacrifice by his people.

Charles G. Finney successfully demonstrated that revival is governed by spiritual laws. The proper use of these laws makes real revival possible. Certainly his contention that when these laws are properly employed revival will result has not been disproved. Failure comes, not because the laws of spiritual awakening are defective, but because men fail to observe and use the laws that make revival certain. Revival today is no less possible than it was in Finney's day. The price is high, for the laws of revival are demanding, but anyone can avail himself of these means.

Prayer is likewise governed by spiritual laws ordained of God. In his providence these laws are part of his divine plan for the good of men. There are some things God will not give his people apart from prayer; not that he is unable to grant them, but because he has ordained prayer as the means by which to obtain them. Man in his relationship to God should think, work, and pray. To substitute prayer when work is called for is no solution, and to work when one should be praying is an exercise in futility. When man has worked and thought as hard as he can, there are still things which cannot be accomplished apart from prayer.

It is erroneous to suppose that prayer is an escape mechanism that frees men from the need to think and work. A Christian student may be anxious to obtain a college diploma. He may and should pray for this coveted prize if it is the will of God. But a lifetime of prayer will not win him the prize unless he takes whatever steps are mandatory to meet the requirements for the diploma. God does not mock the prudential standards of men in order to accommodate his servants. Therefore, a college student should not pray for a diploma without doing the necessary work. He should pray that God will enable him to meet all the requirements. This may, in itself, be the real and true prayer, for by meeting the standards the student will discover that the college is glad to grant him his degree.

The Christian who is ignorant of the spiritual laws governing prayer is dismayed and disheartened when he prays and nothing happens. As a result he often stops praying. Or instead of seeking to discover why his prayers have not been answered and taking steps to correct the situation, he resigns himself to a life of dull indifference in which prayer may or may not be answered. He never knows, nor does he have any assurance, that his prayers will be answered. Such a dismal, lethargic, and self-defeating prayer life is abnormal.

The true servant of God should experience daily answers to prayer. And he will experience them if he faithfully follows God's laws. A simple illustration here might be of help before stating and explaining the laws that govern prayer. The child who inserts a penny in a chewing gum machine will receive a ball of gum for his

penny. Shaking the machine hard before putting in the penny will
yield no gum unless the machine is functioning improperly. The
law of the machine predicates the receipt of the penny before the
release of the ball of gum. If the penny goes into the machine and
no gum is forthcoming then there is something wrong with the
machine. In a limited sense this example is somewhat analogous to
prayer, but with several significant reservations. Prayer is not a
magical or mechanical device. God is not a machine, nor does he
break down. However, when God's children meet the prescribed
conditions of prayer their prayers are answered. Assuming the
proper use of the laws of prayer, the people of God can enjoy a
satisfying and fruitful experience in which answers to prayer are
commonplace rather than rare.

What are the basic laws that govern prayer?

FOR THE GLORY OF GOD

The first law of surpassing importance in the divine order has to
do with the glory of God. All prayer, as well as all acts and
thoughts of life, should have for their chief end the glory of God.
Anything less than this is unworthy of those who claim to know
and serve him. Much prayer falls short of this goal. Even the
mature believer awakens to discover that he often wishes to gratify
carnal desires or bring to pass whatever will fulfill his own egoistic
goals even at the expense of others. Moreover, he sometimes
deliberately chooses his own will in preference to the will of God.
All this does not glorify God. The truly genuine, effective prayer
life must be firmly rooted in the desire to glorify God; the prayer
that is not for his glory will fail since it violates this first law of
prayer.

IN THE NAME OF JESUS

God's Word teaches that prayer must be offered in the name of
Jesus, and this implies two cardinal truths. The first is that prayer
exists for the benefit of those who have been converted to Jesus
Christ. Therefore, for an individual to be on "praying ground" he
must be "in Christ." To be "in Christ" is to be regenerated or to
have had an experience of salvation. It is to have the right to call

God "Father," for the converted person is indeed a child of God. In one sense all men are the children of God by creation. But sonship in the New Testament sense comes only through a personal experience of redemption provided through Christ's vicarious death and resurrection. Unless this kind of relationship has been established, no man is on praying ground. Thus to be "in Christ" and to pray in his name are inescapable necessities, for one to practice effective prayer.

To call conversion an essential prerequisite to effective prayer is not to say that God never hears or answers any prayer of an unbeliever. Since God is sovereign he may deign to answer prayer of the unconverted even when it is not prayed in Jesus' name. This is in full accord with the doctrine of common grace. But it is radically different from answered prayer as it pertains to the believer. The unbeliever can claim no promise from Scripture in which God obligates himself to answer his prayer. Any such answer is indeed the exception rather than the rule. For the believer, however, there are hundreds of promises in Scripture that God will hear and answer his prayers. The Bible is replete with substantial guarantees that the believer in Christ has open doors that are firmly closed to those who do not know the Son of God. God is as good as his Word; he is a gentleman who always keeps his promises. For this reason God's promises to answer prayer are imbedded in the reality of his own nature. Once having sworn in truth that he would answer prayer, if he did not do so, he would be untrue to himself and would be denying himself. But God is true and faithful. Prayer *must* be answered because God is God.

The second cardinal truth is that only the name of Jesus guarantees prayer access to the Father. Therefore, every believer must bring his petitions to God in Jesus' name. His is the name that is above every name and it alone gains us access to the mercy seat of God. Somewhat like the password one gives the sentry at a military post, the name of Jesus alone admits the believer to the Father's presence, and anyone coming without it is considered an intruder. The analogy of the password given to a sentry is not fully adequate, for even a spy can gain entrance to a military camp if he uses the right word. The sentry is not omniscient and cannot discern the thoughts and intents of the heart of another. Before God, however, all things are plain and whoever claims the name of Jesus without the right to do so by virtue of his birth from above deceives only himself. But God is not deceived; therefore, prayer in the name of Jesus without faith in the heart of the one who prays is not efficacious. It will not work.

The Scriptures clearly attest that access to God is through Christ. Paul says: "For through him we both have access by one Spirit unto the Father" (Ephesians 2:18). And again: "In whom we have boldness and access with confidence by the faith of him" (Ephesians 3:12).

ACCORDING TO THE WILL OF GOD

Prayer's third law concerns the will of God. There is no guarantee that God will hear prayer offered contrary to his will. Prayer offered according to God's will is both heard and answered. John observes: "And this is the confidence that we have in him, that, if we ask any thing according to his will, he heareth us: And if we know that he hear us, whatsoever we ask, we know that we have the petitions that we desired of him" (1 John 5:14,15).

Divinely ordained reasons undergird the insistence that prayer, to be effective, must be in the will of God. Finite human beings cannot foresee the future with accuracy, thus this provision is a safeguard against the lack of foreknowledge. When we have evaluated a situation in the light of all the knowledge we possess, we may still pray for that which would not be good for us to obtain, but how can we know this unless we know the future?

Moreover, contained in this particular law is a divine warning for the believer to be on guard against human presumption. He ought not pray earnestly for something he wishes to have when he does not know whether it is the will of God, unless he can thoughtfully and honestly end his prayer with the qualification, "Nevertheless not my will, but thine, be done."

There are some who claim that a petition that is not in accord with the will of God is not a real prayer; that true prayer always is in the will of God. Not so. The most earnest suppliant who ardently seeks God's will cannot always know whether his petition is the will of God. If it is not prayer unless it is in the will of God, he who prays cannot even dare to ask God for anything about which he is uncertain. However, the Christian *can* pray for anything, whether he knows it to be the will of God or not. But he must then present it to God contingently, in the sense that he wants it only *if* it is the will of his Father in heaven.

Profit as well as comfort and hope follow those who pray in the will of God. When prayer is subordinated to his will then all the happenings of life must conform to the promise of the Scriptures that "all things work together for good to them that love God, to them who are the called according to his purpose" (Romans 8:28).

WITH INTENSE DESIRE

The fourth law pertains to the inner heart desires of the one who prays. He must intensely desire that for which he prays. Characteristically much prayer lacks intensity. The prayers themselves reveal the absence of this essential ingredient. When it is present the prayers themselves will evidence it.

Honest inquiry into almost anyone's prayer life will disclose the unpleasant but undeniable fact that the petitions asked of God often are not salted with any great degree of intensity of desire. If one intensely desired the redemption of unconverted friends or relatives, his tears would flow, his zeal to secure their salvation would know no bounds, and his heart and mind would be gripped constantly by this impelling passion. But many things are prayed for once and then promptly forgotten. However, petitions earnestly desired cannot be forgotten nor does he who prays neglect to specify them in prayer over and over again.

Blind Bartimaeus begged the Lord Jesus to restore his sight. He wanted this one thing above all else. The refrain on his lips was, "Thou son of David, have mercy on me." When asked pointedly by Jesus what one thing he wanted, he replied quickly and with fervent desire, "Lord, that I might receive my sight" (Mark 10:46–51). What he desired in his heart, he received, but the answer was related to the intensity of his heart interest and concern.

Hannah, prior to the conception of Samuel, exemplifies intensity of desire, too. The Scripture says she was in bitterness of soul. She wept sore. She poured out her heart before the Lord (1 Samuel 1:10 ff.). All of these external phenomena manifested the passion of her heart as she prayed for a son. Hezekiah was sick unto death when the prophet told him to prepare for the inevitable end. Out of the depths of the intensity of his heart, his tears flowed before God as he asked for an extension of his life. His petition was heard and answered (2 Kings 20:1–3). Prayer that is effective springs from an irresistible and unquenchable intensity which will be rewarded.

Scripture does not explain why God has ordained that intensity of desire should be one of the laws of prayer. No doubt some people think that God should answer prayer whether there is intensity of desire or not. One thing is plain: Just as we accept and abide by the physical laws of nature regardless of their appeal, so we can only accept the spiritual laws that govern us—laws that we did not devise. By them we must live and by them our decisions must be made.

BY ASKING

The Christian sings with the hymn writer, ". . . make all our wants and wishes known." Why does God insist that man make his petitions definite and specific? Men must express their desires, even though God is the all-knowing one. The Word of God declares that he has ordered all things from the beginning to the end, and that the future was known to him in exact detail in eternity. Our tomorrows are known just as our yesterdays were, but still God tells us that asking is an essential ingredient in prayer.

Jesus knew that blind Bartimaeus needed his sight but he made him ask for it. God knew that Hannah wanted a son desperately but she had to ask for him. He was well aware of the armed might of King Sennacherib who threatened the safety of Hezekiah and the independence of his kingdom. Still Hezekiah had to ask God for deliverance. God knew that David was sorry for his many sins but David had to make confession and ask for pardon. It has been and ever will be this way.

Jesus laid down the foundational principle for asking in prayer. "Ask, and it shall be given you; seek, and ye shall find; knock, and it shall be opened unto you: For every one that asketh receiveth; and he that seeketh findeth; and to him that knocketh it shall be opened" (Matthew 7:7,8). Jesus promised that asking, seeking, and knocking would produce results. He did not say that the results *might* come but stated that they *would* come.

Logically, the converse of a proposition is true. The words of Jesus can be rephrased this way: "If you *do not* ask you *will not* receive; if you *do not* seek you *will not* find; if you *do not* knock it *will not* be opened unto you." Scripture throws further light on the subject by asserting that "ye have not, because ye ask not" (James 4:2). Prayer does have numerous complications, but the law of asking is simple enough for the smallest child to understand. Indeed children need no instruction in asking. From the moment they are able to make their wishes known they do so without restraint or reserve and in the greatest simplicity.

Fortunately, asking does not mean that one must write long letters or spend many hours detailing his needs in minute fashion. Hezekiah's prayer for deliverance from Sennacherib is a model for briefness and yet it is comprehensive. Anyone can recite it in less than one minute. His petition for an extension of life can be repeated in less than fifteen seconds. The dying thief who "rejoiced to see that fountain in his day" made his request to Jesus with words that took less than five seconds to repeat. The prayer of our Lord, "Father, forgive them; for they know not what they do," is a classic illustration from the lips of the one who taught men how to pray and who warned, "Use not vain repetitions, as the heathen do: for they think that they shall be heard for their much speaking" (Matthew 6:7).

The value of asking is not to be measured by volubility, or by beauty of expression. Its worth lies in acquainting God with the need, not because God is unaware of it, but because he wants each one to articulate his need as one of the conditions of prevailing prayer.

Psychologically, asking may do something to the one who asks. Its benefits may be directed toward him, and the law itself may have been formulated in part for the values accruing to the asker. When one asks he is confronted with his own problem. Often the knowledge of what he faces has in it the seeds of the solution. Since the answers to prayer are not always outside of man but often rise from within him, this has a salutary effect. But more than this, when he asks he is saying, in effect, that he has come to the end of his own resources and is looking outside of himself to the one who has all power. God may honor this humble admission by energizing within him latent powers of which he had no knowledge.

The Christian must never assume that God made asking a prerequisite to effective prayer for capricious reasons. He may not now or ever comprehend all of God's reasons, but he can rest in the confidence that God never does anything without good and sufficient reasons. The true believer will not advance any explanation that supposes God to be arbitrary, unjust, or irrational. He will not quibble over the rationale of asking but proceed to ask, that he may receive good things from the hand of him who is good in himself.

WITH FAITH

All prayer, to be effective, must be offered in faith. Prayer that is not salted with faith is unavailing. Therefore, faith is an indispensable ingredient for a satisfactory prayer life. The question may be asked whether there can be any true prayer when it is not mixed with faith. The writer to the Hebrews emphasizes the importance of faith when he says; "But without faith it is impossible to please him: for he that cometh to God must believe that he is, and that he is a rewarder of them that diligently seek him" (Hebrews 11:6). James reinforces the argument by warning: "Let him ask in faith . . . For let not that man," (i.e. the man who asks without faith) "think that he shall receive anything of the Lord" (James 1:6,7). Faith appears to be an integral part of genuine prayer.

Throughout the public ministry of our Lord the problem of faith or belief kept bobbing up. Again and again Jesus asked this question of those who sought his help: "Believest thou that I can?" The asking of this question was not something merely mechanical; Jesus expected a certain kind of response. Jesus thrust the petitioners into the arena of faith in which, by conscious choice, they had to make a decision. Luke records the remarkable words of Jesus in reply to the request of his disciples, "Lord, increase our faith." Jesus said: "If ye had faith as a grain of mustard seed, ye might say unto this sycamine tree, Be thou plucked up by the root, and be thou planted in the sea; and it should obey you" (Luke 17:5, 6). It is obvious, then, that faith is an integral element in prayer. But the emphasis of Jesus is not on the quality of faith but on the quantity of it. Faith, to be faith, is always qualitatively the same. Quantitatively it differs widely. Jesus says that even a small quantity of faith will yield rich results. What then will great faith yield, and why do so few possess it?

The end of the quest has not come when it has been established that faith, qualitatively speaking, is an essential element of prevailing prayer. Tell a man he must have faith to believe when he prays and he will nod his head in agreement. Inwardly he may still be puzzled by the unanswered questions: "What do you mean when you say, 'Have faith'? What is faith? How can I get it?"

Faith, as the Scriptures picture it, is a two-sided coin. Both sides of the coin are important. To understand and use only one side of the coin of faith has limited value and will avail little in prayer. Both sides of the coin of faith must be activated.

The first side of faith's valuable coin is the belief that God is able to do what he is asked to do. Obviously it is pointless to ask God to answer prayer if the person praying does not believe God has the power to do so. Someone could read the *Arabian Nights* and rub an Aladdin's lamp, desiring to have himself transported immediately and magically from New York to Cairo. But it is difficult for intelligent and knowledgeable people to believe in jinns or to suppose that if the jinn appeared when the lamp is rubbed that the magical event will take place. It may be a good fairy tale but it's bad theology. Buddhism professes to believe that one who becomes a Buddha is able to go immediately from one place to another. This concept, of course, is rejected by reasonable men. Likewise, the magic carpet of the *Arabian Nights* appeals to the imagination of children and stimulates wishful thinking and captivates the mind of the credulous, but in real life one would wait forever for these fantasies to become a reality. All of these things are nonsense and those who think them real are doomed to disappointment.

When a man petitions God for something, however, he must face the question, "Is God able to do this?" If God cannot answer prayer, then prayer is pathetic and meaningless mumbo-jumbo. If the petitioner asks for that which lies beyond the power of God and he is convinced that it is beyond his power, then it is ridiculous to pray for things at all. Hardly any Christian will admit that he entertains either an agnostic or an unbelieving viewpoint about the ability of God to give him what he asks for. Practically all Christians hold that the power of God is unlimited. They believe that nothing is beyond God's power because he is the sovereign Lord of creation. He who hung the stars in the sky and makes the sun rise and set can do *anything*. He can raise the dead. He can perform miracles. Known laws can be superseded. His power is limitless.

The Apostle Paul had firm confidence that a sovereign God can do anything. Thus he penned his powerful and persuasive doxology: "Now unto him that *is able to do* exceeding abundantly above all that we ask or think, according to the power that worketh in us, Unto him be glory in the church by Christ Jesus throughout all ages, world without end. Amen" (Ephesians 3:20,21).

The conviction that God is able to do anything opens one to endless criticism. Scoffers rise to challenge this viewpoint and demand a variety of proofs. Earnest Christians, too, express hesitancy and sometimes ask whether this notion is biblically sustainable and rationally probable. The rejoinder, of course, is that no one, least of all the biblically oriented student, believes that God can do *anything* without defining what is meant by that proposition and by drawing lines which set it off in a biblical and thus a reasonable framework. Unfortunately, not all people, and particularly not all non-Christians, are acutely conscious of the semantic problem when a Christian asserts that God can do anything. They rashly conclude that when he so asserts he is either a fraud or a fool. In the one case they think he is dishonest; in the other case they conclude he is not worth listening to. In either case they could be right, and in both cases they can be wrong.

To answer the question whether God can do anything, the other side of the coin of faith must be brought into focus. The introduction of this contributing data enables one to arrive at a solution. Only an understanding of the relation between the two sides of the coin of faith makes it possible to believe that God can do anything and at the same time to realize that there are some things he cannot do. Or, if it were to be phrased with more precision, there are some things which God could do but which he will not do. And this latter truth contains the key to the second side of faith in relation to prayer.

Faith believes not only that God is *able* to do what one petitions him to do, but that God is also *willing* to do it. It is the combination of these two that constitutes faith in its generic and biblical sense. One without the other will hardly do. They must exist together. Therefore, when the Christian states that God can do anything, he does not mean that God *will* do everything. There are many things which God will not do, although he is perfectly able to do them. And since he will not do them they may be placed outside the arena of those things which man believes God is able to do in response to prayer. This still leaves an area for prayer which, though now more limited, is large enough to test every spiritual resource in the believer. This we must insist on, however: that God will not grant any request outside the limitations he has imposed —not that God lacks the ability to grant such requests but because he has ordained not to do so.

What are some of the things which God will not do and which therefore are beyond both the scope of prayer and the activity of faith? God has ordained that the earth and the planets should exist in their given forms. Therefore, one should not pray for the sun to stop shining. So long as the earth shall last God has providentially ordered the sun to perform its function and he will not change this although he has the power to do so. And since it is not the will of God, men cannot ask in faith for what he has ruled out as contrary to the divine will for mankind. Likewise, God has created man and given him appetites and laws that govern his physical being. Man cannot pray in faith asking God to allow him to survive without eating and drinking. This prayer is out of bounds. Everyone knows that God could miraculously preserve a man's body without the use of food or drink. But God does not choose to do this. He could have sustained the children of Israel without food during their forty years of wilderness wandering. Instead he sent them manna from heaven. Therefore, the person who ceases to eat and drink for more than a limited time in the false belief that God will sustain him will eventually die. It cannot be otherwise. Even in the case of the miracle performed for Elijah, who went without food for forty days and forty nights, it was only for a limited time. He then returned to the normal routine.

God has given us laws of motion. For one to pray that he may be transported from New York to Paris without recourse to ships, planes or other known forms of transportation is beyond the scope of answerable prayer as we know it. No one has yet reached Paris that way and there is nothing revealed in Holy Scripture that would lead a man to suppose that prayer to this end can be made in faith. It is not in the will of God.

At Pentecost the gift of tongues (glossolalia) was manifested. Men moved by the Spirit miraculously spoke in languages and tongues used by other nations and peoples. Yet today there is no repetition of this miracle. Missionaries who go abroad to preach the Gospel must learn the language the hard way. Some groups emphasize speaking in tongues, but despite this emphasis their missionaries have not received the gift of tongues in the languages of the nationals to whom they go to preach the Gospel. This is not to pass any final judgment on the question whether it is more profitable to speak in a strange and unknown tongue or in a tongue which would be serviceable in fulfilling the terms of the Great Commission. Nor is it intended to rule out speaking in tongues in this age as a genuine manifestation of the Spirit's work.

There still remains an enigmatic problem relative to faith. Suppose one is praying for something about which he is uncertain. He does not know whether his request is in the will of God. He knows that God is able to fulfil it, but he cannot tell whether he is willing to do so. In this contingency he ought to pray conditionally, acknowledging honestly that he does not know whether it is in the will of God, asking that his petition be denied or granted as it pleases God.

The Bible speaks eloquently of men and women who had faith in both kinds; who believed that God *could* and *would* answer their prayers. Several sparkling illustrations from human experience open a window on faith to show believers how others have met and mastered some of life's difficult situations.

Hannah, who has been mentioned previously, is a case study of the principles or conditions of prayer which have been met. The sacred writer depicts her as a woman of a sorrowful spirit, a woman whose appetite had been lost, and the fountain of whose tears had been opened. She besought God earnestly to give her a son. After her prayer in the temple and her conversation with Eli she still had no son. But she left the temple convinced that Eli had spoken the word of the Lord to her and she believed it with all her heart. The evidence of her belief is succinctly stated: "The woman went her way, and did eat, and her countenance was no more sad." The grief of heart disappeared, the fountain of her tears was dried up, and the sorrowful countenance was replaced by radiant joy. She had faith to believe both that God was able to grant her request and that it was his will to do so according to Eli's word from God (see I Samuel 1).

Another illustration is that of Jehoshaphat. The kingdom of Judah was threatened with an invasion by Moab, the Ammonites and the inhabitants of Mount Seir. Jehoshaphat knew that in his own strength he would be unable to emerge victorious against this strong combination of enemies. He sought the face of God in prayer. The prayer itself is a splendid model for praying people to emulate. The basic elements of a good prayer are found in his words, except that the name of Jesus is omitted, but this aspect of prayer had not yet been revealed. When Jehoshaphat finished praying, a prophet brought him a message from God saying that the people of Judah should stand still and see the salvation of their God. Against all of the dictates of human reason they were told to do what appeared to be the wrong thing—nothing. And with the dawning of the day of battle Jehoshaphat manifested his faith first by obeying implicity what appeared to be foolish counsel, humanly speaking, and then by the words he spoke to his people. He cried out, "Believe in the Lord your God, so shall ye be established; believe his prophets, so shall ye prosper" (2 Chronicles 20:20). These were words which sprang from the heart of a man who had faith in God, who believed that God was able and willing to answer his prayer.

Another illustration may be taken from the life of Jesus in whose healing ministry the element of faith was so prominent. He constantly asked those who sought his help whether they believed. On at least one occasion the Scripture says that he could do not great works in that place because of the unbelief of the people (Matthew 13:58). Here was the Son of God—his mighty power short-circuited because it was available only to those who exercised faith. The people who failed to secure the benefits which Jesus was willing to bestow did not lose those benefits because of any lack of desire on Jesus' part to bestow them. Even though he desired to do so, he did not because they refused to believe.

Matthew records the healing of two blind men. They appealed to Jesus in order to receive their sight. They asked him to have mercy on them. But their petition for help was not enough. Jesus delicately probed into their hearts to determine whether they had faith. He inquired of them: "Believe ye that I am able to do this?" and their reply to him was, "Yea, Lord" (Matthew 9:28). In one sense the situation described here is a reversal of faith as it pertains to prayer to God today. We have just finished saying that most people believe that God is *able* or has the power to answer prayer, but the larger problem in the case of the two blind men does not seem to be whether they believed that he was willing, but whether they thought he was able. That is why Jesus asked these men whether they thought he was able, or had the *power* to heal them. We wonder at this difference and ask why Jesus approached it this way. No doubt these men believed that he was willing to answer their petition, and Jesus sensed that they believed. But they apparently had reservations about his power to heal; therefore, he wanted them to affirm that they believed he was *able* to do it. Upon hearing this affirmation of their faith in his ability, he touched their eyes and gave them what they desired (see Matthew 9:27–30).

Other sick people sought help from Jesus and in some of these cases the situation was identical with the problem faced by believers today. The leper who sought for healing came to worship Jesus, exclaiming, "Lord, if thou *wilt,* thou *canst* make me clean." Clearly his dilemma was not whether he had faith in the power of Jesus to heal him. He believed Jesus had that power. His question was whether Jesus was willing to use his power (see Matthew 8:1–3). Jesus responded to the leper and healed him, thus indicating that he was willing to do so. From these illustrations, then, it may be seen that faith includes the conviction that God is both *able* and *willing* to do what is asked of him. Both of these convictions are indispensable elements of effective prayer.

APPROPRIATION

The last law of effective prayer is appropriation. It impinges in some measure on faith and possibly might be included under faith as a third aspect of it. However, it is worth separate consideration and careful analysis.

Faith that believes that God has the power and willingness to do something should produce action in life, demonstrating the reality of that faith. Appropriation supplies this evidence, for it is the substance of things hoped for, the reality of things for which there is, at the moment, no outward or visible evidence of proof (Hebrews 11:1). By this the Scripture means that before the petition has been granted to the senses in experience, it can be viewed as though it were already here. Jesus said: "What things soever ye desire, when ye pray, believe that ye receive them, and ye shall have them" (Mark 11:24). A better translation might be, "Believe that ye receive."

Appropriation counts the answer as though it has arrived, even before it comes. It connotes an attitude of expectancy in which the person who prays waits with a heart of confidence, accepting the gift as though it were already in his possession. When the answer does come he is not surprised because he has already laid hold of it in the biblical sense.

Jehoshaphat's action after his prayer for deliverance from Moab and the other enemies of Judah (2 Chronicles 20) illustrates appropriation in prayer. So far as he was concerned, the victory was already won. Before he moved forward with the people of Judah he had received the answer and no doubts existed in his heart or mind. To him there was the evidence of things not seen but which were both sure and real, albeit still in the future.

A rather indirect yet pertinent example of personal appropriation is found in the experience of Abraham's servant (probably Eliezer) who went forth to find a wife for Isaac (Genesis 24). He prayed and proposed certain conditions. In his prayer he specified that the first woman who would supply him and his camels with water would be the one whom God had chosen to be Isaac's wife. His prayer reveals that he asked God for help in faith. By setting up specific conditions which the woman had to meet he appropriated the answer as though it were already there. But just to be sure that he would recognize the answer when it came he identified the outward evidences that would enable him to discern the will of God without fear of error.

The choice of Matthias in Acts 1 demonstrates the same attitude in prayer. In complete confidence that the answer was forthcoming the apostles cast lots and the lot fell on Matthias. In this same sequence, the events of the day of Pentecost further illustrate the meaning of appropriation. The Lord Jesus had told the disciples to tarry until they were endued with power from on high. They waited for ten days in an attitude of expectancy. They were convinced that the Spirit would come and they were waiting for that coming. They never doubted that the event would take place. Later, in Acts 4, persecution descended on the infant church. The apostles prayed for boldness; and in faith with personal appropriation, consonant with answered prayer, they went forth to testify, and boldness was theirs in actual experience.

These, then, are the laws that govern prayer. Properly understood and correctly used they will revolutionize any prayer life. God has set up the criteria and has revealed to his servants through the Scriptures what they need to know. It is true that there are further qualifications and complications that make prayer less simple than may appear from this discussion of the laws of prayer. This word of caution against oversimplification is needed here because the laws of prayer may be properly employed and difficulties still encountered in getting answers to prayer. Suffice it for the moment to rest the case for effective praying upon these indispensable conditions which must be used if one is to succeed in prayer.

We have seen that life is governed by spiritual as well as physical laws. Prayer has its own set of spiritual laws that control it. Successful praying depends on the knowledge and proper use of these laws. Therefore, effective praying is not simply accident or happenstance. It is possible for all Christians to enjoy fruitful prayer lives and no one becomes a great prayer warrior because he has a special gift. Rather he has acquainted himself, knowingly or unknowingly, with the laws that control prayer, and has developed a skill in their use and an intimacy with God as a result of this skill. Those who unconsciously lay hold of these laws of prayer and who use them properly are surely rare exceptions. All others must dig for their knowledge as they study the Word of God with care. Once they secure the knowledge they can put it into practice, improving and perfecting their prayer lives before God.

V

PROBLEMS IN PRAYER

Prayer has its problems. You may minimize them, avoid them, or pretend they do not exist, but they remain. They stubbornly refuse to vanish into thin air. This is to be expected. Prayer is related to God and while the things of God are oftentimes simple they are sometimes complex. Any relationship between God and men is bound to produce problems. The finite human mind cannot fully fathom the infinite divine mind and God has not given quick and easy answers to all the questions we ask.

The Christian mind tends to oversimplify the problems because of a mind-set that often thinks in opposites or extreme contrasts such as "black-white," "either-or," "yes-no." This mind-set just doesn't see the large areas of gray that are neither black nor white. Just as it is impossible in some situations to assert dogmatically that one course of action or another is right or wrong, so there are no easy and dogmatic answers to the many and difficult problems connected with prayer. This forces us to focus our attention on some of the knotty and hard-to-resolve problems of prayer, and to throw a spotlight on them in order to gain perspective and develop a richer and fuller prayer life. In some instances we can draw definite conclusions and devise specific solutions. In others we may have to wait for further knowledge or qualify the answers since some prayer problems do not yield to orderly and clear-cut anal-

yses or solutions. It is still valuable to face up to problems we
cannot fully solve and for which we do not always have final
answers. We may have to conclude that there is nothing that we
can do except to throw ourselves upon the mercy of God and wait
patiently for the turn of events in the midst of the inscrutable
mystery of his sovereignty.

WHEN GOD ANSWERS "NO"

God answers our prayers one of three ways. He may say "yes,"
he may say "no" and he may say "later." When God says "no" the
very act of denial creates problems for us. Some writers claim that
if you do not receive the things you ask for you have not truly
prayed. By this they mean that it is not true prayer if it is not
answered "yes." The petition was defective, perhaps, in that you
did not pray in accord with the will of God and what is not prayed
in accord with his will is not regarded as true prayer, says this
viewpoint.

First, it is unbiblical to say that you cannot truly pray for
something you know is not the will of God. Also, all of us have
prayed a hundred times asking God for things when we did not
know whether we were in the will of God or not. And in this kind
of predicament such prayer should not be designated "no true
prayer." Scripture itself speaks specifically about both kinds of
prayer and we should investigate carefully what it has to say.

One classic illustration of a petition contrary to the will of God
was the request of the children of Israel for meat on their wilderness journey after they had come out of Egypt. God told them to
be satisfied with the manna he provided day by day. The Israelites
complained about their diet and demanded meat. At that time they
were living under the theocracy; God supplied their food directly.
Their petition was therefore a cry to God for meat even as it was a
complaint against God about manna. Moses says it was "the rabble
that was among them [that] had a strong craving; and the people of
Israel also wept again, and said, 'O that we had meat to eat. We
remember the fish we ate in Egypt for nothing, the cucumbers, the
melons, the leeks, the onions, and the garlic; but now our strength
is dried up, and there is nothing at all but this manna to look at' "

(Numbers 11:4 ff. RSV). The Psalmist makes it abundantly plain that they cried to God for meat. It is equally clear that God granted them what they cried for even though it was contrary to his will for them. Israel paid dearly for that prayer for meat. Heaven indeed was forced and the flesh supplied but along with the gift came the divine sentence: "He gave them their request; but sent leanness into their soul" (Psalm 106:15). Surely the Israelites' demand for meat required the use of extraordinary means. By no ordinary method could the desires of this vast multitude have been gratified. The meat had to come providentially from the hand of God, and it did. The incident teaches us that God does hear and sometimes supplies what is asked contrary to his will. The Israelite prayer was bad prayer, not good prayer. But it was prayer. It should be no surprise to us when God does not give us what it is not his will to grant. What should surprise us is that anyone would pray for that which he knows is not the will of God. This is tragic. In the case of Israel there was a still greater tragedy. They got what they wanted but in the getting they got what they did not want, and they were worse off than they would have been if God had said "no" to their request.

Hezekiah, king of Judah, affords another example. The prophet Isaiah came to him on his sickbed and brought tidings of his death. He said: "Thus saith the Lord, Set thine house in order; for thou shalt die, and not live" (2 Kings 20:1). No plainer words could have been spoken. The message of Isaiah allows for no other interpretation. But Hezekiah would not resign himself to the will of God. Weeping bitterly, he resisted God's will instead of submitting to it. He countered by beseeching God to extend the length of his days (2 Kings 20:2-4). God heard and answered the petition of Hezekiah according to the way he prayed it. Fifteen years were added to his life. As in the case of Israel, demanding what was not the will of God got him what he wanted, along with what he did not want. Manasseh was born in Hezekiah's house during this fifteen years God added to his life. Eventually Manasseh became king. The wickedness of his reign was so great that it would have been better if he had never been born. And he would never have been born had it not been for the desperate plea of Hezekiah, who was out of the will of God. Moreover, during those added years, Hezekiah committed political blunders that adversely affected the destinies of his people.

The second problem of a "no" answer to prayer comes from requests about which we have no certain knowledge whether they do or do not represent the will of God for us. Frequently it is legitimate and necessary to pray "if it be thy will." Who can deny that God's "no" in such an orientation is just as much an answer to prayer as "yes." Of course, we all face the agony of determining whether our petitions have been denied or whether God simply intends to delay the answer. God's delays are not denials, but to discern whether it is delay or denial may be quite difficult in a specific case. But there is no such thing as unanswered prayer. God always answers "yes," "no," or "later."

When we pray not knowing the will of God certainly in a particular circumstance we must be prepared to take what God gives. Scripture contains a wealth of material that thoroughly demonstrates this point. Paul earnestly entreated God to take away his thorn in the flesh. We do not know what that thorn in the flesh was, but we do know that God heard Paul's prayer and answered it in the negative. Paul's plea was not a one-time performance. He pleaded with God for deliverance a number of times before he got his answer. And when the answer came, God said "no." We must allow that "no" can be an answer to true prayer because God told Paul "no" (2 Corinthians 12:7–11).

Shadrach, Meshach, and Abed-nego prayed for deliverance from the fiery furnace to which they were consigned. They knew that God had power to save them but they plainly professed that they did not know whether he would deliver them. They did not know whether they would live or die in the fire. In fact, they did not seem to care particulary. Dead or alive, delivered or consumed by the scorching blaze, they trusted in Jehovah. As they stood before an angry Nebuchadnezzar they answered boldly: "If it be so, our God whom we serve is able to deliver us from the burning fiery furnace, and he will deliver us out of thine hand, O king. But if not . . . we will [still] not serve thy gods, nor worship the golden image which thou hast set up" (Daniel 3:17,18). They prayed for deliverance. But they did not know whether God would deliver them or let them die. What is important is that they were willing to take "no" for an answer because they believed that God does say "no" as well as "yes."

Still another illustration of "no" as an answer to prayer may be found in the experiences of Peter and James in the early church. The church prayed earnestly for Peter's release from prison and these prayers were answered affirmatively. Peter was delivered. We cannot suppose that when James was imprisoned no prayer was offered for his release, yet James suffered martyrdom. God did not choose to deliver him, but he did choose to deliver Peter. In this kind of ambiguity it is impossible for us to explain why God delivered Peter and permitted James to die except to say that it was his will in both cases. Since we do not know the answer, we bow submissively and in resignation to the divine will, confident that our lack of understanding derives from our finitude and not from any defect in the character or outworking of God.

Hebrews 11 depicts the great heroes of the faith. They all had one trait in common. They believed God. The chapter is one of amazing contrasts. One picture presents faithful saints who wrought wonders and experienced miraculous, divine deliverances. The other sketches the anguish of those who were not delivered and who experienced fearful deaths. All prayed and looked to God. Some got affirmative answers to their prayers and others got negative answers ("and these all . . . received not the promise" Hebrews 11:39), proving again that a "no" is just as much of an answer to prayer as a "yes." Some of these saints were delivered from death while others were delivered in death. But whether the answer was "yes" or "no," they were delivered.

We ought to ask ourselves why God says "no" to many of our prayers. The answers may not enable us to tie every knot but they will surely open a window on the divine purposes. Let us assume that our hearts are wholly yielded to God and we want to glorify God, which means that we want his will whatever that may be. If a six-year-old boy were to ask his father to buy him a .22 calibre pistol as a Christmas present it would be most imprudent for his father to accede to the request. Knowing that a six-year-old boy should not be trusted with a dangerous weapon, he would lovingly but firmly refuse to give him what he knows would not be for the best welfare of the lad. At the moment, the boy might not understand his father's actions. He might even be crushed and think his father unreasonable. This is beside the point. The father did what was right, not what was convenient. So God deals with us as a father deals with his child and refuses him what he knows would be harmful.

One of the truly thorny points of tension surrounding prayer comes when we decide whether God has answered our petitions by a "no" or by a temporary delay. More of us have been caught on this seesaw than on almost any other one. I recall vividly the case of one earnest believer who was attacked by a dangerous malignancy. He rejected surgical treatment, insisting that it was the will of God to heal him. Instead of getting better he got worse. An intestinal blockage finally necessitated emergency surgery. The cancer progressed as the physicians forecast and the victim was bedridden. For many long months while he lay dying, the patient persisted in affirming that God was going to heal him. He spoke glowingly and with much assurance of a vision he had had one night in which he thought God promised to double his present life span which meant he would have lived to be ninety years of age. He did not live to be fifty. Death claimed its prey.

From this case study one might gain the impression that the determination to live was so strong that this man sought to force God to give him what *he* wanted, not what God had ordained for his life. The incident does give us a clue to a possible answer to this kind of enigma. God guides not only by his Word but also by circumstances. When we have prayed for healing and have concluded that God has answered our prayers affirmatively, if the circumstances do not bear out our expectations and our apparently certain conviction, then we must reappraise the situation and at least pray, "If it is not really thy will, show us that." However, this prayer must be prayed with open hearts and a willingness to revise our own estimate of the problem, deferring to the will of God.

God providentially allows us, on occasion, to see and to understand why he said "no" to some of our prayers. The passing of the years often reveals to us what was not plain at the time we offered the prayers. Although this has sometimes happened, a question mark still surrounds many of the incidents of life about which we have prayed and God has denied the requests. But while there may be no specific answer, there is a general one. God denied our requests because giving us what we prayed for would not have been for our good. And with this we rest the case.

One of the unforeseen and delightful reasons God says "no" is that he has something better in store. Were he to grant the first request it would then be impossible for the better intention to become a reality. In the life of Elijah God has provided a beautiful example of this principle. Elijah had been victorious in his soul-stirring contest against the priests of Baal. Following the triumph in which his water-soaked animal sacrifice was consumed by fire from heaven and the priests of Baal were slain, Elijah went to prayer. Through his intense prayer activity the three and one-half years of drought were ended and there was the sound of abundance of rain (1 Kings 18:25 ff.). Elijah was flushed by a number of unusual achievements and it would have been natural to expect him to be spiritually invigorated and filled with buoyancy. At this peak in his career he received a message from Jezebel saying that she wanted his head. Elijah lay down in dark despair and urgently prayed for God to let him die: "He requested for himself that he might die; and said, It is enough; now, O Lord, take away my life; for I am not better than my fathers" (I Kings 19:4). For at least two reasons God refused Elijah's request. One was that his ministry had not been completed. There was a work left for him to do. The second was that God had something better than death in mind. Elijah lived on this earth for possibly ten years after he prayed his prayer for death. When the proper time came, Elijah was translated that he should not see death. He was taken alive into heaven: "And Elijah went up by a whirlwind into heaven" (2 Kings 2:11). From this we learn that God's denial may be caused by God's gracious intent to grant a greater blessing.

THE LAW OF INTERNAL CONTRADICTION

One of the problems in prayer might well be labelled the law of internal contradiction. The knowledge of this law helps us to resolve otherwise inexplicable ambiguities. The law of internal contradiction supposes that we pray two prayers and in each petition we ask for affirmative answers to specific requests. When we make these requests our intentions are sincere and honest. There is no known or unconfessed sin in our lives. We pray earnestly and with faith. The contradiction occurs at a level beyond our understanding at the time we engaged in prayer. Unknown to us we are asking for two things, one of which it is not possible for God to say "yes" to without saying "no" to the other. In effect we are praying against ourselves. We do not even know that the one request is opposed to the other. If we did, we would not pray for both, but until we do see this more clearly, we will probably continue to ask for answers to both and become concerned when one answer is "yes" and the other is "no." Then we ask the question, "Why?" Before coming to any conclusion we will be helped by having some concrete situation before us.

I can recall a time in my own life when the Spirit of God was speaking to my heart about a life of holiness. The Scriptures do teach that the people of God should live holy lives: "Be ye holy; for I am holy" (1 Peter 1:16). It is appropriate to pray for a life of holiness. Indeed it is good to pray for holiness at whatever cost, by any road, and through the use of any means. Within a few weeks after offering this prayer daily there came into my experience seemingly undesirable circumstances which occasioned deep heart searching and fervent petition for their elimination. The heart cry for holiness did not abate. Nor did I stop asking for deliverance from the difficulties. Then came that moment of revelation when somehow the question was posed: "My son, did you not ask for me to make you holy?" When answered "yes" there came the second and more devastating reply: "But the disturbing factors you have asked me to remove are the very means by which I am granting your request for holiness. Now, do you wish to be comfortable or do you wish to be holy? For me to remove the circumstances designed to improve your holiness is to preclude the possibility of holiness. Take your choice."

There was a choice to be made. Was the prayer for holiness sincere? Did the desire for holiness, which is always the will of

God for his children, exceed the desire for deliverance from hard circumstances? Of course, the answer is plain. Holiness was the true prayer of the heart and if the hard circumstances were the means by which the prayer for holiness was being answered then the hard circumstances could not be taken away. And who would want them to be taken away? Therefore, we must always be aware of the possibility that there may be an internal contradiction in our prayers. We must accept some of the "no" answers because of this contradiction, and God, who knows the end from the beginning, in his overruling providence distinguishes the real intent of the heart and answers according to that intention. It is legitimate and needful for us to pray for divine enlightment when our hearts are right before him.

THE LAW OF EXTERNAL CONTRADICTION

The law of external contradiction is similar to the law of internal contradiction except that it involves two or more people rather than just one. This may be seen by the following supposition. Let us assume that some employer advertises in the local newspaper for a man to fill a position which carries with it a reasonable salary. Let us suppose further that there are two or more Christians whose qualifications fit the opportunity and each of them is in need of a job. Each one sees the advertisement and all respond to it. Each one prays asking God specifically to give him the job in question. Now there is only one position available, but there are several candidates. Obviously only one of the candidates could be employed. Each, by praying for himself, is praying against the others. God must solve the dilemma. The ones who do not get the job (and maybe none of the Christians do) begin to ask themselves searching questions.

Let us take another case. A large Sunday school has planned its annual picnic. Everyone wants a fair day for the outing. They pray to that end. But the farmers in the surrounding area need rain for their crops. So they pray for rain. Shall God send a rainy day or a fair one? Whose prayer should be answered?

Let us consider an illustration from politics. Two Christians run for public office. Each is convinced that he ought to be elected.

Christians in both parties petition God for their candidate to be elected to the public office. One candidate and one party is bound to lose. How is God to reconcile the opposing prayers?

Take the case of a church without a minister. Quite frequently various members of the congregation entertain opposing views concerning the selection of a minister. Each group prays for its candidate to be chosen as minister. Since only one minister can be selected, the groups supporting other candidates cannot have their hopes fulfilled. How is God to reconcile these differences?

There is a resolution to the problem of external contradiction and it has a negative and a positive side. Negatively, no one should conclude that because a matter did not turn out the way he prayed that therefore the will of God was thwarted. This is a normal temptation, particularly when the individual is convinced that his prayer is in the will of God. The story is told of a teacher in a Christian school who was convinced that Benito Mussolini was the Antichrist. When Mussolini fell from power, this man prayed publicly that God would restore Mussolini to power so that he could play his rightful role as the Antichrist. Such a pose is absurd but it shows how easy we all can be led astray. Since it is consonant with the biblical evidences to believe that in such situations as these the will of God will prevail, we must conclude that when our prayers have not been granted in the affirmative but in the negative, it was not the will of God for the thing we prayed for to come to pass. And inasmuch as other equally sincere Christians were offering prayers diametrically opposed to ours, somebody was sure to be denied his request and find his prayer answered in the negative.

From another angle we should be careful not to assume too quickly that we have the perfect mind of God. Rather, it behooves us all to add to our petitions the phrase, "if it be thy will," and then wait to see whether it is God's will. An attitude of tentativeness is a virtual admission that it is impossible for us always to know the will of God about everything. Therefore, we cannot always pray the prayer of faith with the assurance that our petitions will be granted as we have asked them. To acknowledge that we cannot know the will of God in every case is no defeat in the warfare of the spirit. We trustfully commit our lives to God and we have confidence in him even in those matters about which it is not possible to know God's will. Our faith should not be disturbed, nor our confidence in a prayer-answering God lessened, because of this sort of problem. If we are disturbed, then the fault lies in our ignorance and not in what appears to be the contrary actions of a kind and tender heavenly Father.

THE PROBLEM OF *WHEN* AND *HOW*

God reserves two decisions for himself in answering prayer. They are the decisions *when* and *how* prayer will be answered. If we fail to grasp or if we misunderstand this truth it will cause us an undue amount of difficulty, alarm, and soul-searching. If we probe deeply, most of us find ourselves telling God exactly how we think he should answer our prayers and when he ought to do it. And if God does not do it our way we are annoyed. We forget that some of the loveliest gifts are wrapped in unlikely packagings and we somehow act as though delay of answer is really denial. We will consider first God's *how* of answered prayer and then the timing of answered prayer.

We Christians frequently face financial tensions. This is a common experience. Most of us never have more money than we need. When financial difficulties crowd us it is quite normal to seek the face of God, asking for money to meet our needs. This kind of prayer is legitimate. We are encouraged to pray for financial help. However, one factor should not be overlooked. Perhaps God will choose to answer our petitions in ways we never dreamed of. Instead of supplying us with additional money for what we believe to be legitimate needs, God may suggest that we cut our expenses. Our ideas of what we need and God's idea of our needs may differ. A budget can be balanced only one of two ways. Therefore, it is possible that God may answer our requests for more money by asking us to curtail our expenditures. And when we have done this we will balance the budget. The answer is different from what we anticipated, but it is an answer.

The life of Saint Augustine affords another interesting example of the *how* of prayer. His mother was intensely concerned for the salvation of her son. When she learned that he was going to Rome, she prayed just as earnestly that God would prevent him from going as she prayed that God would convert him. She knew that Rome was a city of wickedness. She thought that nothing but ill could result from his going. Yet God allowed Augustine to go to Rome despite his mother's prayers, and it was at Rome that Augustine found the gift of eternal life in Jesus Christ. Augustine's mother did not know that her son's trip to Rome was necessary to have the true prayer of her heart answered. She did not know he would be converted in Rome. But God knew. So he answered her prayers his way, not hers.

Matthew Henry said that "God's providences often seem to contradict His purposes, even when they are serving them, and working at a distance towards the accomplishment of them." [1] As Henry illustrates, this was true in the life of Joseph. The prayer of his heart was for God to fulfil his vision. He had been given this vision at seventeen years of age, and believed from it that he would be exalted above his brethren (Genesis 37:5–10). What Joseph did not see, and could not see, was that this vision would be fulfilled via a route he would never have chosen. Little did he dream that his brothers would sell him into slavery, nor did he perceive that he must some day be a servant in Potiphar's household. Nor could he have foreknown the wickedness of his master's wife who sought to seduce him. Nor could he have thought this to be God's method for putting him in a dungeon. Nor could he have known that he would meet Pharaoh's butler in the dungeon. Nor could he have known that the butler would be God's instrument to bring him before Pharaoh. Nor could he have dreamed that his appearance before the Pharaoh would result in his becoming one of Egypt's chief leaders. Joseph never would have devised the sequence of events. God did it his way, not Joseph's. The *how* of answered prayer belongs to God. Parenthetically, it should also be said that the timing of the answer was God's decision too. It took more than twenty years for God to bring his will to pass in Joseph's life. At the end of this long process, Joseph himself recognized the finger of God in all circumstances. He said to his brothers, "So now it was not you that sent me hither, but God" (Genesis 45:8).

Christians who have had prayers answered may falsely conclude that God answers similar petitions in similar ways. This is a mistake. God is not limited to answering prayers by any law of uniformity. He delights to do the unexpected. His amazing variety puzzles Christians who have fallen into the rut of regularity. Possibly Moses fell into this rut and sinned against God for that very reason. During the wilderness journey the children of Israel needed water. God told Moses to smite a rock. In answer to Moses' obedience there would flow from the rock all the water they needed (Exodus 17:5,6). By faith Moses obeyed God's command, and water came forth from the rock. Later in the wilderness wanderings he faced a similar situation. This time God told Moses to speak to the rock (Numbers 20:8). The *how* of answering prayer had changed. Moses disobeyed God by striking the rock as he had done previously. May it not be that in addition to his hotheadedness he had concluded that God must work the same way in similar situations? His sin of trying to accomplish God's will in other than God's way resulted in his being forbidden entrance into the Promised Land.

Variety in how prayer is answered may be seen from the ministry of our Lord. He did not follow any set pattern. He healed two blind men simply by touching their eyes (Matthew 9:29). On another occasion he healed a blind man by anointing his eyes with clay mixed with spittle, and then only after the man washed in the pool of Siloam was his sight restored. He raised the widow's son by touching his bier. He took Jairus' daughter by the hand and told her to arise. He stood before the tomb of Lazarus and simply commanded him to come forth. Thus our Lord performed similar miracles by varying means.

God often answers prayer in a fashion quite different from the way we expect. Indeed we may ask for one thing and get another. When this happens our prayers still must be said to be answered, even though we receive the opposite of what we expect. Scripture illustrates this in the life of Paul. Paul wanted to preach the Gospel in Bithynia; instead God slammed the door shut and sent him to Europe rather than to Asia Minor. Adoniram Judson thought he was called to India, but God sent him to Burma. C. T. Studd was invalided home from China to do a greater work in Africa.

Countless Christians have prayed, "Lord, let this woman become my wife," or "Lord, let this man become my husband." And countless Christians have been disappointed when this prayer in its exact form was not answered affirmatively. Later they have rejoiced in the provision of a husband or a wife, but not the one they expected earlier. What they failed to see was that they were praying for a husband or a wife and not for the particular one. God answered the prayer by giving *a* husband or *a* wife but not *the* ones they had prayed for originally. We should not be disappointed when the answers to our petitions are different than we expected. God works this way too.

We face another problem in the timing of an answer to prayer. It is the problem of delay or hope deferred. Some prayers are answered immediately. We all rejoice when this happens to us. Other prayers are not answered at once and despair overtakes us. We begin to question God. We begin to lose faith as doubt creeps in. Let it be remembered from the outset that a delayed answer to prayer is not a denial. All of us will experience many delays as we wait for prayers to be answered. To suppose that all prayers can and must be answered immediately is to misunderstand the teaching of the Word of God. Therefore, we will be less prone to anxiety and unbelief if we accept the fact that delay is part of the divine plan for prayer. We have already alluded to the experience of Joseph who waited more than twenty years for his desires to be fulfilled. Let us look at still other examples from which we can garner valuable lessons.

Lazarus' case is informative. When Jesus was told that his friend was ill he deliberately delayed visiting his home. He waited until Lazarus was dead. When Jesus did come to the grief-stricken home he was greeted by these challenging words from Lazarus' sister Martha: "Lord, if thou hadst been here, my brother had not died" (John 11:21). Perhaps these were words of rebuke. Perhaps they expressed the conviction that the situation was hopeless now that Lazarus was dead. It was too late. This is one mistake we should not make. It is no more difficult for God to raise the dead than it is for God to heal the sick. Yet Jesus knew that Martha and Mary probably thought that while the sick can be healed the dead cannot be raised. His delay may be explained at least in part by this. Certainly Martha thought Jesus would come when Lazarus was ill and she expected him to heal him. When Jesus did come and said to her, "Thy brother shall rise again," she leaped to the wrong conclusion. She thought Jesus referred to the resurrection of the dead at the last day, but instead he had in mind raising Lazarus immediately. Jesus taught these sisters a greater lesson by tarrying than they would have learned had he come to the sick bed of Lazarus instead of to the tomb. His delay was not a denial. It was a boon. They were permitted to see Jesus raise the dead. And their prayers were answered affirmatively.

Paul's prayer for deliverance from his physical affliction also indicates divine delay. His first prayer was not answered. His second prayer produced no immediate response. Not until he had besought the Lord thrice (2 Corinthians 12:3) did the answer come. And the answer, as we have already seen, was "no." It was this negative response that makes the incident all the more compelling. Had the answer been "yes" after Paul had sought God three times, it would be easy to conclude that time was needed to answer the prayer. But since the answer was "no" it appears as though God could have informed Paul of this the first time he prayed. Why, then, did God wait until Paul had come again and again? We do not know, but we can be sure it was for a good reason and that Paul learned a lesson from this experience that he would not otherwise have learned. Perhaps the "no" after much prayer anguish later enabled him to say, "I have learned, in whatsoever state I am, therewith to be content (Philippians 4:11).

Elijah also experienced delay in answer to prayer. He prayed for rain following his victory over the priests of Baal on Mount Carmel. Rain did not come immediately, however. His obedient servant went seven times to look toward the sea. It was not until the seventh time that he spotted the small cloud. Then Elijah sent the message to Ahab about the sound of abundance of rain (1 Kings 18:44). If Elijah, the great prophet of God, had to persevere in prayer and wait patiently before the answer came, it should not be surprising that similar experiences await us.

Daniel, too, was subjected to delay in receiving an answer to his prayer. This episode is beneficial because it introduces a determining circumstance which explains the delay and throws new light on the mystery of waiting for prayer to be answered. When Daniel prayed, God sent his messenger to Daniel immediately. But the messenger was detained for twenty-one days (Daniel 10:11–13). The delay was due to the interposition of Satan's cohorts. A great battle was being waged in the unseen spirit world. God's messenger was detained by an evil being. It was not until Michael, one of the chief princes, came to help him that he was able to leave the scene of the conflict and come to Daniel. This teaches us that prayer does not wing its way to God, nor God's answer wing its way to us, without opposition. God himself may delay the answer, but sometimes delay is occasioned by the forces of evil. They seek to break the power of God and thwart the divine purpose. Satan cannot prevent God from answering prayer. He can, however, get the victory over the one who has prayed by causing him to fall into unbelief. Or he can tempt him to discontinue his importunity when an immediate response does not materialize. We wrestle against principalities and powers—not flesh and blood (Ephesians 6:12). This incident in Daniel's life suggests that even God's timing may be altered by Satan's opposition, although by God's permissive will.

THE PROBLEM OF SECONDARY MEANS

God answers prayer affirmatively by one of two methods. One method is by immediate intervention through the use of supernatural means. The other method is by secondary means or through normal agencies without a miracle. It may be stated as a principle that God usually does not do miraculously what can be done through normal processes. Therefore, the *normal* means of answering prayer is through secondary agencies.

We raise unnecessary problems for ourselves when we insist that God *must* use supernatural means, *i.e.* the direct and immediate interposition of himself into the answer to prayer. An illustration of this is the Christian who, when he is ill, refuses to see a physician. He believes in divine healing and assumes that divine healing demands the immediate intervention of God and the absolute exclusion of physicians. Let us agree that divine healing is found in Scripture. By this we mean that God intervenes directly and he heals without the use of means. But to declare this method to be the *only* one is to limit God in a way he has not limited himself. Nowhere does God affirm that he will always answer prayers for healing by direct intervention even when it is his will to heal. Nor is there anything in Scripture which should lead us to conclude that healing through the use of secondary means (*e.g.* through a physician) is less than a real answer to prayer. Prayer is no less answered when we are healed through the use of medicine than when we are healed without it. The only difference is that God chose to work in different ways to accomplish the same objective. Normally the believer ought to pray for healing and see a physician too, unless he has a special and *bona fide* reason for not doing so.

The lives of men like J. Hudson Taylor and George Müller are informative in this connection. Both of these men operated on what we might call the pure faith principle. They made their needs known to God alone. No human beings were told of their needs. They believed that they had been led of God to look to him alone for the supply of their needs. They did not claim that theirs was the only right approach to the problem, but they did comply in personal obedience to what they concluded was the will of God for their lives. Many and varied answers came in response to their prayers; and in general, God answered their prayers through secondary means. God moved the hearts of individuals to supply those needs. He did not rain down English pounds from heaven, nor did he send manna as he did for Israel in the wilderness. What God did was to speak to hearts and move them to help. And God has always done this even when needs have been made known to men and not to him alone.

THE PROBLEM OF WASTED PRAYER

We ask God for many things that common sense should tell us not to ask for. A moment's reflection would save us from grief about some of them. Even when we know better, the problem tends to repeat itself unless we reflect constantly and ask ourselves the right questions when we pray.

The person who prays to God asking that he may pass an examination *after* he has taken the examination prays in vain. He should have prayed *before* he took the examination. Once the examination has been taken it is too late to pray to pass. What has been written is written. The man who hears of a rich relative's death and then prays, "O Lord, may I be remembered in his will," is making a mistake. If he has been remembered, the prayer is unnecessary. If he has not been remembered in the will, it is too late to do anything about it once the relative has died.

Prayers may be wasted because of a lack of knowledge and this waste may be unavoidable. We may pray asking God to help us locate our missing house keys. If we have only misplaced those keys and they are lying around the house the prayer is not in vain. But if we dropped the keys into the ocean unknowingly and now pray that we may locate them the prayer will not be answered in the affirmative. There are no instances on record where God has miraculously lifted keys from the ocean's bottom. We will have to buy a new set of keys.

A wife may be waiting at the suburban railroad station for her husband to return home, not knowing on which train he will arrive. She can pray while she waits, "O Lord, let him be on the next train." Either he is on that train or he is not. Her prayer is of no avail if he is on another train or is waiting in the city for a train yet to depart. If he is on the train in question, he would have been there whether she prayed or not.

Take the instance of a Christian who had arranged for an automobile to be imported. Having been notified that it had arrived, he went to the dock to pick it up. When he got to the dock the car could not be located. He prayed, "O Lord, let me find my car today." But he did not get his car—then. Unfortunately, it had not been unloaded from the ship, which was now docked in another coastal port. An error had been made. He got his automobile eventually but the prayer at that time was in vain, for the automobile was not on that dock and all the looking in the world would not have located it there.

In this sort of incident it is not a true solution to say that God does not answer prayer or that God said "no" to the prayer. When such prayers do not yield fruit, the Christian should seek to understand the reason why and not permit such experiences to decrease his faith in God or in prayer. Prayer is reasonable and operates in accord with the general realities of life.

There are other useless or wasted prayers said naively by Christians who wrongly jump to the conclusion that "all things are possible" as though that phrase were unconditional. It *is* possible for God to change a man into a woman but he *is not* going to do so. It *is* possible for God to restore the ten thousand dollars in bills which were destroyed in a fire, but there *are no cases* on record where he has done so. William Carey would have been delighted if God had given back to him the precious manuscripts that were destroyed in a mission fire in India. Instead, Carey had to do the work all over again. It is possible for God to enable a missionary to speak the language of the people he is trying to reach, without having to learn that language the hard way. But I know of no instances where a missionary has been given the permanent gift of a language without having to learn it. Even those denominations which stress speaking in tongues acknowledge that their missionaries have to learn foreign languages. It is possible for God to impart a knowledge of physics and chemistry to a man immediately and intuitively without the benefit of obtaining such knowledge through the normal learning processes. However, there are no cases on record where men have gotten this knowledge without diligent study. It is possible for God to keep the gasoline tank of the missionary's automobile filled by supernatural means in an isolated and remote field where no gasoline is available. But it does not happen that way.

The lesson we all should learn from these illustrations is this: just as God has ordained that some things may be secured by prayer, so God has ordained that there are some things which must be secured by other means than prayer. This does not rule out the proper use of prayer, but it keeps prayer within its rightful limits. The missionary can pray, "Lord, help me learn the language," and God will do that. Carey could pray, "Lord, help me remember and rewrite the materials which were destroyed in the fire," and God will do that. The man who lost his house keys may pray, "Lord, help me get the situation clarified," and God will do that through his securing another set of keys. Let each of us be sure that there is no wasted motion by praying for things we ought not ask for.

THE WILL OF GOD

We all have prayed for things we have felt sure were the will of God. Then we have been dismayed by our failure to receive what we asked for. We did not receive something else in its place. We received his answer in the negative. This type of experience can be utterly devastating. Undoubtedly, many sincere Christians have suffered traumatic injuries from which they have not recovered. As a consequence they have ceased to pray or their prayers have become ineffectual. How may we approach this problem and what explanations are there for such an experience?

The first principle that sheds light on this riddle is the truth that if something is the will of God the petition will be granted. This precept is supported by John's teaching that "this is the confidence that we have in him, that, if we ask any thing according to his will, he heareth us: And if we know that he hear us, whatsoever we ask, we know that we have the petitions that we desired of him" (1 John 5:14,15). When we have prayed believing that our prayers are in the will of God, and we do not receive affirmative answers, the first question we must ask ourselves is: "Was it really the will of God?" In most instances we will have to confess that it could not have been the will of God. We were mistaken about God's will. Instead of praying as though it were the will of God we should have prayed, "If it be thy will."

There may be another answer to the same problem. We have seen that success in prayer is restricted by our knowledge of, and our obedience to, the laws which govern prayer. Perhaps the petition was the will of God contingently, subject to the fulfillment of the terms ordained by God for prayer. This means that the answer did not come, not because it was not the will of God, but because of our failure to meet the necessary conditions. There may have been unconfessed sin in our lives. Perhaps we had an unforgiving spirit. Maybe we lacked faith. Maybe we evidenced no importunity, and failed to manifest intensity of desire. In this event the failure to receive what was requested may be laid directly at our own door and we ought not blame God.

In considering this complexity we must avoid one error at all costs. It is the error of concluding that God is at fault—that there is something deficient in him whether it be his love, his power, or his intention. God is not, and cannot be, at fault. The difficulty must always be outside of our Father in heaven. "No good thing will be withhold from them that walk uprightly" (Psalm 84:11). "Heaven and earth shall pass away, but my words shall not pass away" (Matthew 24:35).

Since the root of the riddle here is the question of the will of God, it affords an occasion to restate the methods by which we can find out the will of God for us. In general it may be said that there are three ways by which the will of God may be ascertained. We can know it from the Word of God itself. We can know it from circumstances. We can know it from the inward persuasion of the Holy Spirit.

The will of God may be known directly and indirectly from the Bible. The Scriptures speak directly about such things as tithing, holiness, salvation, etc. God is not willing that any should perish. Therefore if we perish it is not because God wills it. God commands us to tithe (Malachi 3:8–10). Therefore if we do not use our money according to the known will of God we walk in disobedience to the divine will. God commands us to be holy. If we do not seek to fulfill this command we are going against the revealed will of God. Indirectly the will of God may be known by what might be called the accident of Scripture. Perhaps we casually turn to some portion of the Word of God when faced with a difficult decision. God speaks to us from that portion of his Word even though it may be taken out of the context.

We may know the will of God by circumstances. God opens doors and he shuts them. He prepares the way before the feet of his children. If God shuts a door we can know that this is not the will of God. If God, in response to prayer, opens a door we can know that this is his will. It is reckless to press open doors that

God has shut. And it is foolish to refuse to enter doors that he has opened.

We can be guided by the Holy Spirit. As we pray we are drawn into communion with the Holy Spirit. His still small voice witnesses to our spirits concerning the will of God through the Word of God. This kind of guidance is, of course, subject to abuse. But we should never surrender the possibility of its usefulness when properly oriented, even though it has its dangers. These then, are the ways by which we can know the will of God. Is there anything which can be added to this by way of further guidance? The testimony of George Müller which appeared in a tract indicates the helpful method he used in discerning the will of God.

1. I seek at the beginning to get my heart into such a state that it has no will of its own in regard to a given matter. Nine-tenths of the trouble with people generally is just here. Nine-tenths of the difficulties are overcome when our hearts are ready to do the Lord's will, whatever it may be. When one is truly in this state, it is usually but a little way to the knowledge of what His will is.

2. Having done this, I do not leave the result to feeling or simple impression. If so, I make myself liable to great delusions.

3. I seek the will of the Spirit of God through, or in connection with, the Word of God. The Spirit and the Word must be combined. If I look to the Spirit alone without the Word, I lay myself open to great delusions also. If the Holy Ghost guides us at all, He will do it according to the Scriptures and never contrary to them.

4. Next I take into account providential circumstances. These often plainly indicate God's will in connection with His Word and Spirit.

5. I ask God in prayer to reveal His will to me aright.

6. Thus, through prayer to God, the study of the Word, and reflections, I come to a deliberate judgment according to the best of my ability and knowledge, and if my mind is thus at peace, and continues so after two or three more petitions, I

proceed accordingly. In trivial matters, and in transactions involving most important issues, I have found this method always effective.

One final word must be added. If we are truly convinced that something is the will of God and there are no time limitations which make it obvious that fulfillment is impossible, our only recourse is to continue steadfastly in prayer for the specific item. George Müller spoke of petitions which he had been making for more than twenty-five years, which had not yet come to pass. But his conviction that these were the will of God was so strong that he intended to persevere in those petitions until they were fully granted. But in those instances where we are convinced that we know the will of God and yet circumstances disprove this conviction there is only one thing left to do. We must assume that it was not the true will of God. Thus if any one of us thinks it is the will of God for him to be elected to a public office and when the votes are counted he finds he has been defeated, he must then conclude that it was not the will of God. Or he may conclude that he failed to fulfill the conditions required by God if he is to answer prayer. But in no event should God be held responsible nor should one's confidence in him be impaired, since the failure is at the human, not the divine, level. This discussion of the will of God leads to still another problem in prayer, the problem of faith.

PRAYER AND FAITH

Prayer without faith is like faith without works—virtually useless. This we have already said in our discussion of the laws that govern prayer. Faith is linked to the will of God in prayer too. If we do not have the conviction that the petitions we ask for are the will of God then we must add to our prayer the qualification, "If it be Thy will." But all of us have prayed "believing" that it was the will of God and still have been disappointed when our petitions have been denied. Since we sincerely, albeit wrongly, thought those petitions to be the will of God we have been dismayed by the results. One of the best antidotes to our dismay is a proper understanding of faith. If we had this understanding it might have

prevented the problem from arising in the first place. And in order
to dispel the difficulty we must first distinguish between "the gift of
faith" and the "grace of faith."

Paul states that the "gift of faith" is one of the gifts of the Holy
Spirit (1 Corinthians 12:9). Some have this gift and some do not.
The Holy Spirit confers it on an individual as a gift in general, or
he gives it in specific instances. If we do not possess the gift of faith
this does not mean we are living a sub-standard Christian life any
more than the man who has not been given the gift of tongues or of
interpretation. The possession of the gift of faith does not make us
better or worse in the sight of God, nor does its possession mean
that we have been given the gift because we are worthy of it. It
comes from the Holy Spirit according to his sovereign good pleasure and he bestows it upon whom he chooses.

The gift of faith may be exercised in numerous ways. One has to
do with physical disease. If we pray for a man who appears to be
dying and beyond the help of medical science we have no way of
knowing whether we can pray for his recovery in faith unless we
have been given the "gift of faith." Scripture nowhere promises
that this or that sick person will or will not recover from his
sickness. Since there is no promise in the Bible which we can claim
for healing in such a case we can only pray, "If it be Thy will,"
unless there is the "gift of faith." The healing or the death of the
sick person is not related to unbelief and thus to sin. If we do not
believe he will be healed we are not sinning, nor does this imply
the absence of a faith we ought to possess. If we think we have the
gift of faith and the petition we were expecting God to answer is
denied, then it is apparent that we did not have the gift of faith. If
we had had the gift of faith the petition would have been granted.

The "grace of faith" differs from the "gift of faith" in several
ways. The "grace of faith" is available to all and belongs to all. If
we do not have this kind of faith it is sin. This is so because the
"grace of faith" is based upon some promise from the Word of
God. Therefore, the absence of the "grace of faith" is sin. We do
not need to receive the "gift of faith" to believe those things which
have been promised. We only need the "grace of faith" which is
available to all of us. When we pray for peace of heart and mind

and do not have faith to believe this petition will be answered, it is sin for there is a promise to that effect (Philippians 4:5–7). If we pray for the necessities of life without faith to believe that God will supply them, this is sin for there is a promise to that effect (Matthew 6:33).

We may conclude that whenever we present any petition which can be anchored to a promise in the Word of God, the failure to exercise the "grace of faith" is a sin. We ought to be able, and are able, to have faith for these matters. But when we are faced with a petition about which the Word of God affords no light as to whether it is or is not the will of God we must look to the "gift of faith," the presence or absence of which is not sinful. The sole basis on which we can claim the promise for those petitions for which there is no biblical warrant is by the "gift of faith." We should be most careful, however, not to presume or to use the idea of the gift as a means to twist the arm of God to force him to give us what we want but which is not his will.

RATIONALIZATION

Christians as well as non-Christians use rationalization to offer creditable explanations without adequate analysis of our true motives. We employ it to explain away prayer problems which trouble us or truths we do not wish to face. Rationalization is a form of self-deception, a kind of logical illogicality. However devoted we are to the Lord Jesus Christ we undoubtedly use rationalization unconsciously in our thought processes. Quite naturally, most Christians would deny and deplore conscious rationalization as a tool of deception. It is more frequently than not an unconscious driving force which permits us to escape from that with which we do not wish to grapple honestly and forthrightly. Therefore, we must engage in self-examination to help us prevent the use of this escape device. A few illustrations will permit us to see some of the forms that rationalization takes.

The minister of a church asks a layman to teach a Sunday school class. The layman does not wish to take the responsibility. He is not remotely interested in it, nor does he really care whether it is the will of God for his life. Inwardly he knows that he will not finally accept the assignment. Outwardly he assumes a cloak of impeccability by assuring the minister that he "will pray about the matter." He has no intention of praying about it in any genuine sense at all. He is using a polite method of telling the minister he is not going to take the job. He justifies this action subconsciously by rationalization. If he were to examine his heart fearlessly and face the issue frankly, he would realize that if he had been brave enough, he would have refused then and there! He would not have used this fictitious recourse to insincere prayer.

Another devious form of rationalization is to use Satan as a scapegoat for our own failures. It sounds very spiritual. A student may fail to study for an examination, blaming Satan when it is simply his own laziness. A preacher may blame Satan if his sermon does not click, when the real reason for its failure lies in his careless preparation or lack of prayer. Satan certainly is directly responsible for much of this world's woe, but he ought not be blamed for some of the defeats we suffer in life's battle and for which we ought to shoulder the full responsibility. Because of our defective human nature we always seek to find a scapegoat in order to whitewash ourselves and to point the finger of suspicion elsewhere.

One way for us to avoid the hard work, the sacrifices, and the cost of securing answers to prayer is to say as piously as possible: "It is not the Lord's will." When we say this it can be translated to mean that we do not desire intensely what we have prayed for. Or we do not welcome the blood, sweat and tears required to attain an objective that calls not only for the power of God but also for human effort and energy. Or we grow weary of waiting for the answer to come and falter for fear of having to "pray it through." Or our faith is faulty and we resort to this pious fraud to cover our own sin. This is not to suggest that it is always wrong to use the expression "It is not the will of God," but to make certain that we use it sparingly and only after we have searched our hearts to be certain that it is not indeed the will of God.

Another classic way of applying a similar phrase is to say, "I don't think the Lord would have me do this." Translated more accurately it means, "I don't want to do it." We use this tack to gain the sanction of deity and to assuage our own sense of guilt. The fact that we have failed to consult God or include him in the decision-making process is thus neatly glossed over. Our halos remain intact.

Of all people, we Christians should face the problem of unanswered prayer fearlessly. We should earnestly try to find in ourselves the reason for our failure to secure what we have asked. We ought to avoid using rationalization as an escape from reality, for all we do is deceive ourselves by this specious method of covering up what should be made plain. God and men are not fooled.

THE PROBLEM OF LOGICAL FALLACY

Christians marry but not all such marriages are fully Christian. Marriages may be made in heaven but they are lived out on earth. Rare are the partners who do not need time to adjust to each other. Indeed the failure to adjust accounts for many marital breakups. When Christians get caught in a paralyzing web of circumstances involving marital problems they properly resort to prayer in a serious and determined effort to find a solution. They discover to their chagrin that prayer, *per se,* does not always yield a direct solution, and in many cases it was not intended to do so. It is often a means by which other forces may be set in operation to bring relief. In these situations, Christians experience frustration and need more insight into themselves and their own conduct when they pray.

Take the case of the man who prays that God will make his wife easy to live with. He prays this prayer honestly and sincerely because his wife really is hard to live with. He prays fervently because he is quite convinced that she is at fault. It does not occur to him that he might be blameworthy. He probably never gave this a thought and would be deeply shaken if anyone suggested that his wife's attitudes were a predictable response to his own actions. She has become, in part, what he has made her to be by his own conduct. When he prays for God to make her easy to live with he might also ask God to show him if there is anything in his own life which produces an undesirable reaction in his wife. He might say it this way: "What is there in me that calls forth this response?"

Another common household problem is marital coldness. A man may pray that God will deliver his *wife* from this unfortunate condition. But he may never relate his own conduct to her unresponsiveness. He may be totally blind to the fact that his own actions lead to his wife's hostility, causing her to fail to respond to him. When he prays for God to deliver her from *her* problem he should be praying for God to change *him* too. The logical fallacy in this, as in so many problems, is for the individual to assume the sanctity of his own conduct and blame his partner, when the fault really lies on his own shoulders. But if he sees no need to change or is unwilling to change there is little likelihood that his wife will change. And when she does not change, he concludes that God has not answered his prayers. He still does not see that his problem lies within himself. Therefore, he who prays should anticipate that God may need to do something to him and in him, in order to grant his petition.

Furthermore, we all know that some true believers are abnormal or maladjusted. Neurotic, they need treatment if they are to be delivered from themselves. While God can deliver such people from their bondage by a miracle, he also works through the secondary means of a psychiatrist or a psychologist. These abnormal Christians may be praying Christians; however, they cannot pray aright because they are abnormal. They generally have no insight into the fact of their illnesses. They think they are wholly normal. Their responses are "normal" in the light of their illness, but abnormal in the light of general conduct. These illnesses take many forms. Some victims have Messiah complexes. They play God. No one can shake them from their conviction that they have the mind of God, and that anyone who disagrees with them must be wrong. They then become the hounds of God. They pursue to the death those who do not follow their prescriptions. How shall we pray properly for such people? What results can we expect in response to our prayers?

When a man loses an eye or a leg we do not pray that God will replace the lost member by a special miracle. There is nothing in the Scriptures to give us ground for such hope. Christ did heal a man with a withered hand. He did make the blind see. But there appear to be no accounts in sacred Writ or church history in which men have had lost limbs replaced. In man's psychological makeup there is a sense in which he can suffer a traumatic injury comparable to the loss of a limb. This man will always suffer from the effects of such an injury. He can be helped. He can learn to appreciate his problem and make the best of his loss. But he may not be rehabilitated as though there never had been an injury. We should thank God for the splendid services of those who are able to probe the human mind and bring to light the forces which affect man in his inner being. And we should expect God through prayer, by the use of these secondary means, to bring help and healing to these sick souls. And if God ordains that there be no healing, we must bow to providences even as we bow to them when Mongolian idiots and mentally retarded children are born.

We who are not so afflicted should be sympathetic and understanding of those who are. Spastics, for example, are not contrary minded. They do not wish to be this way. They desperately want to be normal but never quite make it. The abnormal and the maladjusted must be accepted as they are. They must be helped if this is possible. But it is unrealistic to suppose that a man cannot be abnormal because he is a Christian. And it is equally unrealistic to suppose that all such people will be cured by prayer alone. Once again the resort to secondary means as part of the prayer solution is essential. On the other hand, if God chooses to intervene miraculously and directly, that is his prerogative, although he does not ordinarily do so.

THE PROBLEM OF EVIL

Sooner or later all praying Christians must come to grips with the problem of evil. The good citizen prays for good government. He works and votes for good men, but wicked men are elected to public office. He believes that alcoholism is a great evil. Therefore he works and prays to remove this scourge of man from his nation. But it is not removed. He sees in some foreign country a ruler who stands opposed to what is holy and in accord with the will of God. He prays that God will remove him from power. But God does not, and when the evil despot dies he is replaced by someone who is no better than his predecessor, or is actually worse.

This brings us full circle to the primary question. Why does God allow evil in the first place? Surely it is not his will, and if it is not his will and we pray for that which is the will of God, why are our prayers not answered the way we would expect them to be answered? We cannot dispute when God says "no" to requests that are not good for us. We can understand this. But when we pray for the elimination of evil and we feel sure that the result would be good for everyone and must be in accord with the will of God, and yet the prayer is denied, then we are faced with a greater problem. What is the answer?

We must rest in the assurance that God is sovereign and that man exists for the purpose of glorifying God. Since this is true we should pray the prayer of resignation, "Thy will be done." We should confess that we do not know exactly how God goes about to accomplish his own purposes and bring about his own glory. But we accept the fact that God permits evil and intends to bring good out of it. The true prayer of our hearts is for the glory of God and this is answered. God even uses evil to attain his ultimate objective. Moreover, the results of our prayers for the destruction of evil may be thought of more as delays rather than denials. Many have prayed for the victory of God over evil and have died without seeing it come to pass. But ultimately; evil will be destroyed. At that time every prayer of every saint for the elimination and defeat of evil will have been answered in the affirmative.

PUTTING OUT THE FLEECE

One of the familiar Old Testament incidents of guidance, prayer, and the will of God is the story of Gideon whose experience points up several problems we all face sooner or later. Earlier in this chapter we discussed the difference between the gift of faith and the grace of faith. Where God has spoken, the grace of faith operates. It is sin if we do not believe God when he has spoken. But we may pray for many things without knowing the will of God. Sometimes God gives us the gift of faith which shows us that the petition is his will. However, we also offer petitions for matters

about which there is no promise of an affirmative answer from the
Word of God and there is no gift of faith to believe God. Sometimes it is possible for us to rest in faith saying, "If it be Thy will."
But this does not help when we are praying about a decision which
must be made immediately one way or another. The road to the
left or the road to the right must be taken, but we have no specific
promise from the Word of God. We are not granted the gift of
faith as evidence by which to choose. Forced to make a choice, we
may resort to the device of "putting out the fleece."

The use of the fleece for guidance comes to us from the story of
Gideon. Some may question whether Gideon did the right thing.
God had already called him. He told him that he would smite the
Midianites through him (Judges 6:16). When the time came to
battle against the enemy, Gideon evidently wanted to be absolutely
certain that he was in the will of God. So he put out the fleece
(Judges 6:37–40). God honored his request, and responded to the
terms and conditions laid down by Gideon himself. When the
terms and conditions were met by God they became the basis for
Gideon's decision to battle against the Midianites. It is futile to
argue whether Gideon's conduct was spiritual or unspiritual. Certain other conclusions are quite plain, however. Gideon asked God
to guide him by circumstances. God honored his request and gave
him the guidance he asked for and by which his actions were
determined. Gideon accepted what God sent and began his cam-
paign against the Midianites in the light of it.

From this story it seems fair to say that there are times and
circumstances when the use of the fleece is a legitimate method for
determining the will of God. Certainly it should not ordinarily be
used as a device for discovering the will of God until other
methods and means have yielded no decision. When faced with a
choice that cannot be postponed, and when there seems to be no
other form of guidance, then the fleece may be put out. It presupposes, then, that we have already used prayer and the Word of
God first. It also presupposes that when we put out the fleece we
do so with honesty of heart, evidencing a true desire to know what
God would have us do. It also presupposes that we are willing to

do whatever God shows us to do through the fleece. This form of commitment may be found in the Scripture, "He that sweareth to his own hurt, and changeth not" (Psalm 15:4). What kind of fleece should be put out depends upon the individual and God. It must be something which is reasonable and which leaves us with peace of mind as we wait for the answer. A few examples may be of help.

Let us suppose one of us becomes convinced that God wants him to start a new work which will ultimately require a hundred thousand dollars. He wants to be absolutely certain that it is the will of God and not just the will of self. He does not get clear guidance by any other method. So he puts out the fleece asking God to send him five thousand dollars as a token that this project is his will, and he sets a deadline. If the money comes in before the deadline he goes forward. If the money does not come in, he relinquishes his dream as of self and not of God.

Suppose a minister has a certain parish or a businessman a certain job. In his heart he concludes that God wants him to make a change. Yet he does not wish to make this known to anyone for fear that he may be running ahead of God. So he goes to prayer seeking God's help as he puts out a fleece. Perhaps he sets a deadline asking God to open another door by that time or else he will conclude that God wants him to remain where he is. If no doors are opened he stays where he is. If something does open up he moves in that direction.

Caution should be employed in using the fleece, since it is subject to carnal abuse. Other means must be exhausted first. It should be a last resort. Above all its dignity should not be casually destroyed by thinking of it as a mechanical device. Thus it has been misused by some who have tossed coins to decide the will of God. "Heads I do. Tails I don't." And this with the pious prayer that God should determine which way the coin should fall!

THE PROBLEM OF FEELING

We all have experienced moments when our prayers have been influenced by moods and feelings. Sometimes the mood has been

joyous, spontaneous, effortless, and soul-shaking. At other times it
has been dry, dull, lack-lustre, and a burden. Sometimes words
have gushed forth as from a fountain while at other times nothing
has come or the words have been halting and broken. Watts
suggests that we need to beware of what he calls the nimble
mentality. With or without joy, with or without fast flowing words,
with or without spontaneity, prayer must go on. Prayers are not
answered according to feeling, or nimbleness of mind, or facility of
expression. However, we often experience a sense of depression
and defeat when our times of intercession are marked by moods.
The absence of joy and spontaneity makes us feel as though we
have not succeeded. We rashly conclude that our efforts have been
wasted. God has not heard. Such conclusions are erroneous indeed,
for feeling should not be allowed to defeat us.

The prayer of J. Hudson Taylor helps to define this problem
more clearly, and to place it in proper perspective. He was asked if
he ever prayed without consciousness of joy. His reply was, that
often his heart felt like wood, but frequently most wonderful
answers came when prayer was a hard effort accompanied by no
joy.

The picture of Christ in Gethsemane is not one of joy and
spontaneity. The scene itself is stark and oppressive. The night is
dark. But the darkness is spiritual as well as physical. As he
wrestles alone, the Lord's agony is accompanied more by desola-
tion and sorrow than by joy and triumph. Yet his prayer was
abundantly answered. He was strengthened physically. He emerged
triumphant from Gethsemane to stand before Pilate and Caiaphas,
and at last to be crucified on Calvary's tree.

> 'Tis midnight; and on Olive's brow
> The star is dimmed that lately shone;
> 'Tis midnight; in the garden now,
> The suffering Saviour prays alone.

> 'Tis midnight; and for others' guilt
> The Man of Sorrows weeps in blood;
> Yet he that hath in anguish knelt
> Is not forsaken by His God.

There will be dark and cheerless hours of prayer. There will be those moments when the forces of darkness tie our tongues, fetter our feet, dull our vision and impair our sight. But we are to pray on, for in these moments God may visit us with responses undreamed of and give victories long sought for. It is always too soon to quit praying, even when praying is the last thing we seem able to do.

THE LAW OF GEOMETRIC PROGRESSION

The combined prayers of many of God's people yield a tangible harvest beyond computation. The power generated through the prayers of one believer may be increased as others of us add our petitions to his. Jesus declared that if two agree as touching anything and ask God for it, it shall be granted them (Matthew 18:19). Curiously enough the Greek word used here is the one from which the English word *symphony* comes. The word itself may be translated *to sound* or *speak together*. Jesus did not say that one hundred must be agreed. Nor fifty. He asked for two. This is no disparagement of numbers by Christ. Rather it indicates that if as *few* as two are in agreement they can shake the world for Christ. When two people do get together and pray in harmony the results will be staggering. What most of us forget is that God has a law of geometric progression which operates according to the number of people who pray.

The law of geometric progression differs from the law of arithmetic progression. In the latter the addition of more people increases the power in direct proportion to the number involved. But the law of geometric progression makes it possible for more people to increase the power at a greater rate. Thus the Scripture promises to the people of God, "Five of you shall chase an hundred, and an hundred of you shall put ten thousand to flight" (Leviticus 26:8). If we compute the power arithmetically, if five can chase a hundred, then one hundred should chase two thousand. But here one hundred chase ten thousand. Each one of the five chases twenty. But each of the hundred chases a hundred. The law of geometric progression is in operation. The power increases five times as much for the hundred. Of course, we do not claim that this is a fixed law so that the proportion remains constant. But it does express a great truth which is often overlooked. The greater the number of people who gather together to lay hold of God, the greater the resultant power beyond what the added numbers would normally indicate. Robert E. Speer wrote: "But if fifty men of our generation will enter the holy place of prayer, and become henceforth, men whose hearts God has touched with the prayer-passion, the history of His Church will be changed." [2]

CONCLUSION

Problems in prayer should stimulate and challenge us, not alarm and defeat us. Above all they should not keep us from prayer. Nor should they lead us to underestimate the mighty power of prayer. Grappling with prayer problems opens the way to a more effective and efficient life of prayer.

We all must remember that answers to prayer are not ends in themselves. God uses prayer to educate his people and to produce holiness of character in them. The education and holiness of his people are the ends in view, not simply answers to prayer. God does use prayer as a supreme means by which these objectives are accomplished. Therefore, the believer should use prayer with an eye to what God's ultimate objectives are. Then and then alone will prayer be seen in proper perspective and from it will come the maximum results.

We all see through a glass darkly; there is much that we do not understand. We should seek to enlarge our understanding and push back the barriers to knowledge. The source of truth remains unchanged, to be sure. We always have the written Word of God. Our understanding of the truth increases as we gain new insights into the Word of God. However great our insights, we can never exhaust God's revelation of himself, but we must enlarge our knowledge of it and test our opinions by it. Finite men have no final word to write. Every age will disclose problems undreamed of before. New insights will be required for the guidance of God's people as the eternally relevant Word is applied to new circumstances. This is as it should be, even as we believe that the principles underlying prayer will endure for all ages.

Notes

[1]*Matthew Henry's Commentary on the Whole Bible* (New York: Fleming H. Revell Co.,) Vol. I, p. 215.
[2] Robert E. Speer, *Missionary Principles and Practice* (New York: 1902), p. 479.

VI

HINDRANCES TO PRAYER

The road to spiritual competence in prayer is beset by many hindrances. What these are and how they may be overcome are matters we should deal with realistically. Identifying and overcoming the hindrances will bring them to a timely end. The failure to do this will keep us shackled and enslaved. What are some of these hindrances which prevent us from maturing as prayer warriors and from attaining the goal of a victorious prayer life?

INDOLENCE

Plain laziness is a vital hindrance to effective prayer. There is more than one kind of laziness, however. I may be indolent in the sense that I am lazy about everything and this is a hindrance. Or I may be indolent in the sense that while I am not slothful about other things I am lazy in prayer. A college student who rarely studies may be an outstanding athlete who is exceptionally hard working on the football field. He is diligent in sports but indolent in study. The man who is totally lazy may appear to be worse off than the one who is lazy only in prayer, but the net result is the same in either case. Both are ineffective.

We can quickly grasp the meaning of diligence in prayer by observing the example of our Lord Jesus. In the Garden of Gethsemane, Luke says of Jesus that "being in an agony he prayed more earnestly: and his sweat was as it were great drops of blood falling down to the ground" (Luke 22:44). Someone will immediately ask whether this is a fair sample for comparison because Christ is God, although it can be postulated that he was praying as man in the Garden. But the example of Christ the perfect prototype is not the whole story. He is not the only one who was diligent in prayer. There are other excellent examples of devoted men who were human and not divine. They should be listened to when we consider indolence.

Elijah is a splendid example. James says that "he prayed earnestly" (James 5:17). The Greek phrase might better be translated: "he prayed in prayer." Many Christians "say" their prayers. Elijah "prayed" his prayers. For him it was serious business. It is no wonder that his prayers produced a drought for three and one-half years, and that at the end of that time his prayers brought rain to the parched land. Elijah was never careless or casual. What he did, he did with zeal. Perseverance and industry were the hallmarks of his life and when he prayed and when he acted he did so decisively. The majestic figure of Elijah is a marvelous model as he enfolds his body in his mantle and settles down to pray for rain after the long drought. He prays earnestly again and again. There is no sloth, no easing off, no respite from the labor. Here is man hard at work and accomplishing a task.

Paul commended Epaphras whom he described as "always labouring fervently for you in prayers" (Colossians 4:12). This Scripture is luminous because the Greek word for "fervently" is the one from which the English word "agony" is derived. It comes from the same root word which described Jesus in Gethsemane as "being in an agony." Moreover Epaphras was not one who prayed once and ceased to pray. He "laboured fervently for you in *prayers.*"

> Go when the morning shineth,
>> Go when the noon is bright,
> Go when the eve declineth
>> Go in the hush of night;

> Go with pure mind and feeling,
> Fling earthly thoughts away
> And, in thy chamber kneeling,
> Do thou in secret pray.
> —Jane C. Simpson

IMPATIENCE

Patience is a virtue praised by many, possessed by few, and sought only occasionally. We pray and want an immediate response. We either do not know or do not care that God has ordained that *when* and *how* our prayers will be answered are decisions which belong to him alone. God may delay in coming but he never comes too late. And God may send an answer to a prayer by wrapping it in a package we do not recognize. Many of us are impatient and fret anxiously either because we do not recognize the answer God sends or because it does not come at a time we think it should.

God enjoins us to "wait patiently for him" (Psalm 37:7). James says that "the trying of your faith worketh patience" and the word *patience* can be translated *endurance*. We insist that God should act immediately. We desire, yes, even demand, the answer *now*. God intends to respond, but he has other objectives besides the answer to the prayer itself. The answer *is* a blessing but there are more blessings wrapped up in his gift than the specific answer to the specific prayer. Not the least of the added blessings is the patience we so sorely need—patience that can be developed better only as we experience delay in answer to prayer.

Another reason for delay is that God needs time to answer prayer. This may sound as though we are imposing human limitations on a sovereign God, but such is not the case. Certainly God does not need time when he intervenes supernaturally. Through a miracle the time factor can be eliminated. But God most frequently works through ordinary channels and this takes time. Since God has chosen to work generally through ordinary rather than miraculous means, it may be said that he needs time to answer prayer. The person who prays must then follow the example of the farmer who sows. The farmer patiently waits for the seed which he has

sown to bring forth its harvest. Likewise, prayer is a seed which is
sown and which, in its proper time, will bring forth its good fruit.
Just as the impatience of the farmer will not hasten the growth of
his corn, so the impatience of the Christian will not hasten, and
indeed it may hinder, the time process used by God as he answers
his prayer.

HYPOCRISY IN PRAYER

Hypocrisy may be conscious or hidden and unperceived. In
either case, it destroys our effectiveness in prayer. Jesus drew
attention to the sin of those who "love to pray standing in the
synagogues and in the corners of the streets, that they may be seen
of men" (Matthew 6:5). Their primary purpose was not to converse with God but to give men the impression that they were
conversing with God and to secure the plaudits of men by making
them think they were religious people. Christ announced that the
secret chamber with its closed door is preferable. But his premise
was not intended to stamp out spontaneous public prayer before
men. He wanted to condemn the abuse of public prayer when it
was employed hypocritically—a strategy used by pious frauds to
gain a reputation of an earnest saintliness they neither possessed
nor deserved. Entering an inner chamber and closing the door is
not an effective method for conquering hypocrisy unless transgres-
sors change their hearts. Only inward transformation will cause
them to change their outward practice.

There is a hypocrisy of another variety that creeps into prayers
that some of us pray before men. It is subtle in its orientation and
deadly in its consequences. Underlying this hypocrisy is the assumption that we can somehow put God on the spot and so force
him to give us what we pray for. We use this device in public
prayer, conveying an implied necessity on the part of God to give
us what we have asked for. We even thank God publicly for the
answer and presume to believe that the answer is on the way. Since
men have heard our prayers and praises, we conclude that God is
somehow obligated to grant us what we want lest he lose status
before men. We resemble the child who makes a scene before the
guest in the home, demanding and receiving what he would never

have dared ask for nor would he have received if no guests were present. Despite our loudest disclaimers, this form of hypocrisy crops out more frequently than we are willing to admit.

LACK OF IMPORTUNITY

"It's always too soon to quit." As a cliché this is good. In the life of prayer it is easier to talk about this than it is to practice it. Yet no amount of rationalization will pull down the wall which comes between us and God when we fail to persevere in prayer. Call it earnestness, importunity, perseverance, prevailing in prayer, or what have you, it is the absence of this attribute which keeps us from praying through successfully.

The early church prayed resolutely for the deliverance of Peter from jail (Acts 12:5). Here the translation "prayer was made without ceasing" would be rendered better "prayer was earnestly being made" for Peter. But the correction in the translation does not invalidate the need for importunity. The saints did pray continuously and with perseverance. In fact, when Peter appeared following his deliverance they were still praying (Acts 12:12). The Acts of the Apostles repeatedly reflects importunity in many of the prayers which are recorded.

Christ spoke two parables in which he stressed importunity. In the case of the importunate friend he pictured a man who knocked and continued to knock at his friend's door until he received bread (Luke 11:5–10). In the parable of the unjust judge the widow worried and harried the judge until she obtained justice. The latter parable fully accords with Jesus' teaching "that men ought always to pray, and not to faint" (Luke 18:1–8). Jesus did not say, however, that God the Father is like the friend who did not wish to get out of bed, or the judge who was unjust. God is not like either of them. He wants to bless. He wants to answer prayer. He delights to do exceeding abundantly above all we can ask or think (Ephesians 3:20). Why then is importunity necessary?

God's plan included importunity for our sakes. By it we demonstrate our sincerity and earnestness. By it we learn more of the mystery and wonder of prayer. By it we are purified and perfected. The man who knocks and runs away is not serious. The man who asks and then forgets is not in earnest. But the man who prevails is the man who pleads and persists. Let us thank God for the privilege of praying importunately.

A DEFECTIVE HOME RELATIONSHIP

Tension and friction in the home between husband and wife can be a hindrance to effective prayer. Apparently the Apostle Peter knew of such an instance when he commanded, "Likewise, ye husbands, dwell with them according to knowledge, giving honour unto the wife, as unto the weaker vessel, and as being heirs together of the grace of life; that your prayers be not hindered" (1 Peter 3:7). No doubt in this particular situation the husband was at fault in treating his wife in a manner which hindered him in prayer. It hardly matters whether the obstacle arises between husband and wife in their relationship to each other or in relation to their children. Nor is it necessary to pinpoint whether one or the other is at fault or both of them. As heirs together their disunity has hurt their effectiveness in prayer.

When I am angry with my wife or she with me we cannot pray together in concert. We cannot pray in the Spirit who is grieved and quenched by such disharmony. Moreover Scripture says, "That if two of you shall agree on earth as touching anything that they shall ask, it shall be done for them of my Father which is in heaven" (Matthew 18:19). But when my wife and I are at odds with each other we cannot be agreed, either in our personal devotions and relation to each other or in our common prayers. It is necessary to right the wrong relationship first.

We ought not to suppose that the marital relationship is the sole source of prayer friction. A lack of concern and consideration for people outside the home can result in the same loss of power. My relationship to other people, then, is an important factor in effective prayer.

CIRCUMSTANCES

Circumstances are frequently permitted to be an external hindrance to successful petition. This is true because we are prone to reason and to examine events and draw conclusions. When we do this, faith finds its backing more in the way we read the circumstances than in the power of God. When we ask God for something which we think he is capable of supplying, it is easier to pray and to have faith than when we ask for something which is circumstantially impossible. In the former case we confidently expect an affirmative answer because human reason sees no difficulty. But in the latter situation when we ask for what seems to be humanly impossible, we convince ourselves there is no way out of the impasse, and therefore we either conclude that God cannot get around it, or we are doubtful that he can. And so we pray according to our opinions of the relative possibilities from the human perspective. Somehow we lose sight of the truth that it is not more or less difficult for an omnipotent God to answer prayer. Omnipotence knows no limitation. There are no degrees of relative ability to do anything. We can question whether something is the will of God, but there can never be a question whether something is beyond the power of God. Nothing is beyond his power. If he can answer any prayer, he can answer all prayers. The magnitude of the request is immaterial.

Money is one of the circumstances which profoundly influence our lives. Somehow we find it easier to trust God for a dollar than for a hundred thousand dollars. In theory, of course, the well-instructed Christian with "head" answers would deny that there is a difference. In practical experience most of us would have to admit that there is a difference depending on the amount of money involved. This attitude which allows circumstances to affect us hinders prayer. The amount we need should make no difference, all other things being equal.

The solution to the problem of circumstances lies in the Word of God. When circumstances overtake us and loom so large that we stumble, it is due to a deficiency of faith. Therefore, we must seek greater faith, and the road to more faith leads straight through the Word of God, for "faith cometh by hearing, and hearing by the Word of God" (Romans 10:17).

IGNORANCE

We often cease praying when we do not receive quick answers to our petitions from God. Discouragement overtakes and assails us. Here the hindrance to effective prayer is our ignorance. Prayer, as has been shown, is governed by spiritual laws. The failure to be acquainted with or to use these laws properly does produce disappointment. We are not speaking of those laws which govern prayer such as asking, believing, and receiving. There are still other laws to which reference must be made. And it is advisable to work down from the obvious to the less obvious by way of illustration.

God is both omniscient and omnipresent. He knows all things and he can be everywhere at the same time. Man does not share these attributes of God. Therefore, for a man to pray that he may be in two places at the same time, or to ask God to give him infinite knowledge, is patently foolish. All things are *not* possible, nor does the Scripture which says this (Mark 9:23) mean what some people seem to think it means. What is clearly not the will of God is not possible, and it is not God's will for men to be omnipresent or omniscient. We may ignorantly ask God to grant us these two requests but we will never receive an affirmative response.

This illustration is easy to see. After all, who has made any mistake along this line? But what about the little girl who stops to play on her way home from school and falls in the mud? Her mother had forbidden her to do this, but she did it anyhow. The girl asks God to clean the stains from her dirty dress so that her mother will not be angry with her. Obviously, she does not understand the operation of the law of cause and effect. As the little girl sowed so shall she reap. She sowed in disobedience and must face the consequences. Even this is easy to see. But what about the little boy who *accidently* tears his pants? He knows his mother will be angry, yet he had done nothing to deserve her anger. There is no real guilt on his part. Fearful of the consequences he asks God to fix his torn pants. We will not say that God is *unable* to restore torn pants. But it is far more likely that needle and thread will do the job, and unless there are other factors in such a situation, who would encourage the little boy to ask God to restore his pants to the condition they were in before the accident occurred? He might better be told to pray that his mother will accept his innocence as she wields a needle instead of a paddle.

Perhaps more frequently than we care to admit we think naively that God will do what he simply has never promised to do and never will do. Because we are ignorant of this fact we cease to pray when disappointment overtakes us. We must always ask ourselves whether we are expecting something we have no biblical reason to expect. We need to dispel our ignorance and come into the fuller light of God's way of working. His ways are not our ways (Isaiah 55:8,9), and we must accommodate ourselves to his ways, for he will not accommodate himself to our ways without abdicating his godhead.

Ignorance may be conquered several ways. One way is to search the Scriptures and learn what God really has said. The second is to subordinate human reason to the divine will. The third is to allow the Holy Spirit to guide our hearts in prayer so that we may be restrained from asking what we have no right or warrant to ask for. Certainly the Scriptures are silent about many matters, and the cultivation of the spiritual sensitivity under the influence of the Holy Spirit becomes important as we seek to adapt our desires and requests to the will of God.

REBELLIOUSNESS

Rebelliousness is just another name for self-will—"*I* want what *I* want when *I* want it." This hindrance takes two forms, one of which is linked to importunity. It is possible for importunity to become self-will. This is the sin of insisting on the gratification of my own desires whether God wants it that way or not. It is the resolute pursuit of getting what I want even when God has indicated that I should accept "no" for an answer. Importunity ceases to be importunity when it insists upon having its own way against the known will of God. The consequences of importunate rebelliousness are always unpleasant and frequently disastrous.

The second form of rebelliousness springs from discontent with my present condition. The sky will not always be blue and the birds will not always sing. There are dry deserts to be traversed and prison cells to be endured. In any circumstance of life I should be able to pray effectively, for effective prayer does not depend upon the outward condition. But when, because present circumstances are not to my liking, a spirit of rebelliousness creeps in, then effective prayer eludes me. The heart that kicks against the pricks cannot pray, but when I accept the outward circumstances as God's present provision, he gives me a peaceful heart that becomes the prayerful heart.

Usually rebelliousness springs up when I am not truly convinced that the will of God is best. Sometimes it comes when my spirit rejects authority because I wish to remain autonomous and not feel obligated to anyone. Whatever the reason for it may be, rebelliousness evidences a defect in my relationship with God and it is certain to create a stumbling block to effective prayer. The cure for it is the surrender or yielding of self without reservation to God and the willing acceptance of the will of God for my life.

LACK OF WORK

We cannot ask God to do for us what he has ordained we are to do for ourselves. A popular slogan attributed to Dwight Lyman Moody says, "Pray as though you had never worked, and work as though you had never prayed." There is a measure of truth to both sides of this maxim. One does not exclude the other. Both must be harnessed together for the glory of God. We are called upon to pray and to work. Sanctified common sense shows this to be true.

Imagine the college student who prays to pass an examination and then does not study the subject matter. Imagine the man who prays for God to make him a physician and then does nothing to obtain the education essential to the practice of medicine. Imagine the Christian college unitedly praying for regional accreditation and then doing nothing to meet the standards by which accreditation is measured. Now it is undoubtedly true that there are items for prayer, the answers to which lie completely outside of human agencies. Some circumstances shut us up to prayer alone. But most of life brings prayer and human effort together so that one without the other spells defeat.

In the prophecy of Isaiah there is the classic example of Israel crying out to God, "Awake, awake, put on strength, O arm of the Lord" (Isaiah 51:9). God replies to this cry for help by saying, "Awake, awake; put on thy strength, O Zion . . . Shake thyself

from the dust . . ." (Isaiah 52:1,2). Prayer to God for help was
fine. But this was the time for the people of God to do something
for themselves. And there seems to be adequate justification for
suggesting that we should not ask God to do for us what we are
able to do ourselves. Prayer *and* work, then, are essential except in
those circumstances which clearly dictate that one of them alone is
all we are required to use.

If I am out of work I should pray and then go out to look for a
job. If I would pass an examination I should pray and then study
for the examination. If I wish to write a book I should ask for
divine help and then proceed to do the necessary research and sit
down to write out the results. If I see a girl I think is the will of
God for me to marry I should begin courtship. Prayer and effort
through faith in Christ can do almost anything. But prayer without
effort often is a stumbling block. And effort without prayer is to
trust in self alone when faith in God and prayer are needed.
Therefore, all of us ought to combine work or effort with our
prayers and we will be surprised what God will do.

FAILURE TO WATCH

When a nation is at war, the sentry who falls asleep on duty is
court martialed. He is supposed to remain alert and awake. To
sleep is to shirk one's duty. In the army, no matter how desirable
sleep may appear to be and no matter how extenuating the circumstances, the one who falls asleep is derelict in his duty. Christians,
like sentries, are commanded to watch. They are also commanded
to pray. Indeed they are commanded to watch *and* pray.

The Scriptures tell us about impulsive Peter at the first celebration of the Lord's Supper. There in the quiet of that moment our
Lord prophesied that the sheep would be scattered when the
shepherd had been smitten (Mark 14:27). Peter was quick to
respond. Certainly there is nothing in the account which would
lead us to conclude that Peter was insincere. He was no hypocrite
as was Judas Iscariot. It was his sincere intention to identify
himself in the suffering of his Master. He cried out honestly and
with a sense of genuine commitment, "If I should die with thee, I
will not deny thee in any wise" (Mark 14:31). Later that night

Jesus took Peter, James, and John deep into the darkness of Gethsemane's Garden. He did not ask them to die with him or for him. He only asked them to watch and pray with him in those moments of agony. And they fell asleep. They did not watch, and because they did not watch they did not pray.

In the Upper Room, Peter had acted as the spokesman for all of the disciples. All had agreed that like Peter they would die with Jesus. So it was when Jesus finished his prayers in the Garden he came out to find the three disciples asleep. And he spoke to Peter, "Simon, sleepest thou? couldst not thou watch one hour?" Surely these were not words of rebuke and condemnation. Jesus understood Peter's frame and remembered he was dust. They were words which searched Peter's heart, however, and drove home the lesson that watching is essential to prayer; that the failure to watch leads to the failure to pray. Then it was that Christ gave the commandment which shall endure for all generations, "Watch ye and pray, lest ye enter into temptation. The spirit truly is ready, but the flesh is weak" (Mark 14:38).

Why did the disciples of Jesus not watch with him in that dark hour? Why did they fail?

"First, because their willpower gave way in the crisis. They had not counted on so long or so hard a road. There were reproach and hazards of which they had never dreamed in those evenings by the Sea of Galilee, when the sun was all a glory of red and yellow over the Judean hills. Although willpower is not as strong as subtle instinctive forces within us, nevertheless there are times when only iron restraint can save us. General Gordon, who met his death in the Soudan beneath the spears of the Mahdi, was once led to a room full of treasure and told by high Chinese officials that this treasure would be his if he would countenance certain dishonourable practices. Iron will, developed in desert marches, in fighting disease, and in upholding the Empire's honour in three continents, came forward to save him and gave him power to refuse. There are unexpected tests, crises for which no one is prepared, temptations for which no one has developed a specific defense; and, when the rush of circumstances is upon one, all one can do is to fall back in determination upon a former dedication and pray for strength to hold fast.

"Again, they failed Him because they were unable to share His dreams. There was no set to their minds to carry them onward in the midst of the gathering storm, and they slumbered and slept, insensitive to the immense significance of the night in the life of Jesus. They did not realize that for the sake of His dream of a new era in human existence Jesus committed His all, and God's all, to a farcical trial and a savage crucifixion as the utmost which love could do in redeeming men. The sheer unthinking dullness and the inability of His friends to use their imagination hurt Jesus more than all else. It was a time for great friendship, and Jesus received vacillating indifference. . . . But His disciples did not lose the battle that night; they had lost it long before. Their action on the fatal evening had been prepared for in previous weeks. What we think today we shall do tomorrow; what we are at twenty we are apt to be at forty, only more so. Weeks of spiritual slackness, even if in the presence of Christ, had made easy their action on Jesus' night of agony. . . .

"Not only did their wills and their dreams give out, but also their belief. They had lost faith in themselves and left Jesus alone without their presence. . . . But on this ghastly night these men, who could have meant so much by their mere companionship, had no confidence in themselves. They had lost sight of what they had to offer of friendship in His hour of tribulation." [1]

The disciples of Jesus did not pray. They did not pray because they did not watch. And they did not watch because willpower gave way, burdens were not shared, and faith failed. If we are to pray we must watch. And if we are to watch we must become people of iron will. We must catch a vision and dream dreams of Christ's empire and His dominion from sea to sea. We must have faith in the dream and vision. Then, and only then will we both watch and pray.

UNCONFESSED SIN

Unconfessed sin in my life is like water poured on a fire. It quenches it. The Psalmist said: "If I regard iniquity in my heart, the Lord will not hear me" (Psalm 66:18). This must be linked up with 1 John 5:15, "And if we know that he hear us, whatsoever we ask, we know that we have the petitions that we desired of him." The logic of this is unassailable. When we have known, unconfessed sin in our lives, God will not hear. If God does not hear we will not receive the answers to our petitions. It is as simple as that. Scripture elsewhere affirms this principle. Isaiah says (59:2): "But your iniquities have separated between you and your God, and your sins have hid his face from you, that he will not hear." Zechariah wrote: "Therefore it is come to pass, that as he cried, and they would not hear; so they cried, and I would not hear, saith the Lord of hosts" (7:13).

Unconfessed sin is more than a mere handicap to effective prayer: it is a dam which blocks the petitions until the obstruction which produced the dam has been eliminated. Sin has to go. Scripture states that "If we confess our sins, he is faithful and just to forgive us our sins, and to cleanse us from all unrighteousness" (1 John 1:9). Isaiah says, "Seek ye the Lord while he may be found, call ye upon him while he is near: Let the wicked forsake his way, and the unrighteous man his thoughts: and let him return unto the Lord, and he will have mercy upon him; and to our God, for he will abundantly pardon" (55:6,7). When there seems to be some block and prayer goes unanswered the first question we should ask ourselves is whether there is unconfessed sin in our lives. The existence of sin is frequently the reason for ineffectual prayer.

There is a good reason why sin in our lives renders us impotent in prayer. If God were to overlook sin and give us what we pray for he would do violence to his own being. He would be acting inconsistently and his attribute of holiness could be called into question. Moreover, it would be difficult to accept the biblical teaching that God will hold the unrepentant and unbelieving responsible. For if he hears and answers the prayers of his children despite their unconfessed sin, why should he not also justify the unregenerate despite their sin? The holiness and righteousness of God require that he not overlook sin even in his redeemed children. Although they have standing before God because they have been justified, yet their unconfessed sin is a bar to fellowship and effective prayer just as the refusal to receive Christ is a bar to justification. It is foolish to expect God to honor our prayers when there is known, unconfessed sin in our lives. In order not to be hindered in prayer we should confess and forsake all known sin.

LACK OF FAITH

James speaks about the "prayer of faith" (5:15), and Paul about the gift of faith (1 Corinthians 12:9). All of us know that our prayers must be salted with faith. But knowing this, and achieving it, are two different things. Nobody who has worked at prayer seriously can say that he has always prayed in faith. All of us have been wanting in faith from time to time. Sometimes we have "prayed in faith" for one petition and have lacked faith for another at the same time. Whatever our experiences have been, both Scripture and the facts of life teach that the lack of faith is a hindrance to prayer.

We should see that the *lack* or insufficiency of faith does not necessarily mean the *absence* of faith. There is a vast difference between them. The simple act of prayer is in itself a sign of faith. There is hidden in any prayer some measure of conviction that God is and that God will hear. The prayer itself may not be changed with strong faith. Indeed faith may be anemic and relatively insignificant. The hindrance more often than not is a complicated one. Rarely do we face the choice between "no faith" and "full faith." Usually it is a choice between "small faith" and "great faith." Moreover, we must distinguish between that petition in which we pray knowing the will of God and the petition in which we do not know God's will. In the latter situation we can rest in full faith that God will answer "yes" or "no" according to his will even though his will is not known and thus we have no faith to believe that what we ask is his will. In the former situation we may fully believe our petitions to be in the will of God and still not have "strong faith." Our chief point of concern here is not with the petition in which the will of God is not known. Rather it has to do with our lack of faith for those requests when we think we know the will of God and still do not have the degree of faith that ought to be present.

There are two steps we can take when we seek the faith we know we do not possess. First, we must pray honestly, "Lord, I believe, help my unbelief." This often removes the difficulty and God graciously grants faith and assurance in the Holy Spirit. The other step is to search out the promises of God in Scripture. Whatever God says is true and whatever he promises will be fulfilled when the conditions are met. Therefore, we must find faith through the Word of God, as has been intimated earlier.[2]

It is possible for all of us to have strong faith. God plays no favorites. Strong faith has a volitional element in it and we must exercise our wills in this regard.

> Faith, mighty faith the promise sees,
>   And looks to God alone;
> Laughs at impossibilities
>   And cries, "It shall be done."

Faith has its trials but these work patience (James 1:3). Satan tries to work havoc with our faith and so undo the work of Christ. He calls into question the veracity of God. He seeks to implant doubt and despair in our hearts. He magnifies unfavorable circumstances beyond their true proportions. But we who are God's people can resist these attacks and continue in faith despite them. Indeed these adversities may become the very means by which faith is tested and by which it grows stronger and sturdier.

> Trust Him when dark doubts assail thee,
>   Trust Him when thy strength is small;
> Trust Him when to simply trust Him,
>   Seems the hardest thing of all.
>
> Trust Him! He is ever faithful;
>   Trust Him for His will is best;
> Trust Him, for the arms of Jesus
>   Are the safest place of rest.

> Trust Him through the cloud and sunshine,
>   All thy cares upon Him cast;
> Till the storms of life are over,
>   And the trusting days are past.

WRONG MOTIVES

Prayer is hampered by wrong motives. We search our hearts as
we ask ourselves the question, "Why do we want this?" We must
grant that it is difficult, if not impossible, for us to examine
ourselves so thoroughly that we can always discern our hidden as
well as our obvious motivations. Beneath the exterior of each of us
there is the man that men know him to be, the man that his wife
knows him to be, the man that he knows himself to be, and the
man that God knows him to be. Each one of these men is different.
Men do not see me the way my wife sees me. My wife does not see
me the way I see myself. And I do not see myself the way God sees
me. God alone sees me as I really am. There are aspects of myself
of which I have no knowledge. They are hidden from me. Hence I
can never know my motives perfectly. But I can know them well
enough in a general sense to prevent obvious troubles. In those
circumstances where my own motives are hidden from myself, I
can expect God to overrule for his glory as I submit myself to him
in faith.

James suggests that sometimes we ask for things so that we may
consume them upon our lusts (4:3). This is our carnal nature in
operation, seeking those things which cater to the flesh. God denies
us these petitions because we ask amiss.

There are requests which center purely in self-interest. Perhaps
we want to be choir soloists, purportedly for the glory of God,
when it is really for the praise of self. Maybe we seek high
ecclesiastical offices (for he that desireth the office of bishop
desireth a good work [1 Timothy 3:1]) but the reason for desiring
this form of service may be to glorify and to promote ourselves
before men. Maybe we want better jobs with greater responsibility,
ostensibly so that we may make a greater contribution to the
business or industry we are in, but the real reason is that we want
more money and do not care particularly how we attain this

objective. Maybe we ask God for larger and more expensive homes together with more leisure time, not that God will be glorified through them, but that we may live indolent lives.

It is possible for Christians to pray sincerely for hardship, suffering and martyrdom and to do this, not for the glory of God, but in order to satisfy a subconscious, neurotic compulsion to suffer, all the while thinking their motives are genuine expressions of a desire to glorify God. A neurotic individual may actually enjoy or get intense personal satisfaction out of suffering. While he may give the outward appearance of self-abnegation and glorious patience under the tribulation, his desire to suffer may be equally as selfish as the desire of a man for a better home, and absence of suffering.

Someone has said, "There is the reason a man gives you and then there is the real reason." Whoever gives the wrong reason as an explanation for his action has either deceived himself or he is dishonest. Dishonesty indicates a defect in moral character in addition to the fact that in all probability it was wrong motivation which caused the dishonesty in the first place. Deception of self may spring from no evil intention, but usually such deception is subconsciously designed to justify a questionable motive. Therefore, it is imperatve for us to search our hearts to discover our true motivation so that our prayers may not be hindered. Whether the person who prays knows or does not know that he is asking amiss, the result is the same.

> And so my prayers he hears and heeds,
> Mindful of all my daily needs;
> Gracious, most gracious, too, in this—
> Denying, when I ask amiss.
> —Luella Clark.

FORMALITY

There have always been differences in the Christian world on questions of liturgy and formality in worship. Sincere men have disagreed sharply about matters of vestments, order of service, use of musical instruments, gowned choirs, liturgical responses, use of incense, etc. This problem spills over into our prayer lives too. We soon discover that the repetition of religious phrases or mere lip devotion does not improve our prayer performance. Indeed, prayers of this stripe quickly become meaningless. We can say the Lord's Prayer a hundred times without effect and the net result can be worse than not praying at all. In the course of repeating a formal prayer we may have embraced practices and fallen into habit patterns which will have to be reversed and unlearned. A clergyman friend told the story of one woman in his congregation who was the mother of four children and the proud possessor of a doctor's degree. But she was thoroughly dissatisfied with the prayer life of her family so she came to him for help. His inquiry into her personal prayer practice revealed that her nightly routine consisted in repeating the child's prayer, "Now I lay me down to sleep." Her prayer was a routine formality. She needed little help to convince her that what she did was quite immature, and she eagerly accepted guidance as to what she should have been doing.

What makes prayer formal and unavailing is the use of words without the heart. Jesus said: "But when ye pray, use not vain repetitions, as the heathen do: for they think that they shall be heard for their much speaking" (Matthew 6:7). He was striking out against outward formalism divorced from heart reality. John Bunyan said, "In prayer it is better to have a heart without words than words without a heart." [3] Prayer should not be an empty formality but a living, vital, dynamic reality combining words and heart.

It is easier to repeat a short memorized prayer, or even to read one from a book, than it is to formulate a new one and bring to bear the mind, the heart, and the will in a deliberate and meaningful context. Of course, informal prayer rarely matches the beauty of a well-constructed prayer written by one who has literary gifts. But God nowhere indicates that he is concerned with the excellence of our prose or poetry. He looks upon the heart and its intention. Formality toward God is a handicap, not a help. This does not suppose that God can be approached irreverently. Whoever comes is always a suppliant who must have a humble and contrite spirit.

Formalism is always a bar to effective prayer. It is something every Christian can do without.

AN UNFORGIVING SPIRIT

An unforgiving spirit works like a termite. Such a spirit harbors enmity against a brother for real or fancied wrongs. Whether the wrong is genuine or not, the harboring of this spirit in the heart undermines prayer's foundation. Christ commanded us to be reconciled to our brother *before* we bring our gifts to the altar. The estrangement must be overcome, the block to effective prayer must be removed. Only then can the gifts for the altar be offered in good conscience (Matthew 5:23–25).

Jesus said, "If ye forgive not men their trespasses, neither will your Father forgive your trespasses" (Matthew 6:15). When Peter asked Jesus how often he should forgive a brother who had sinned against him, Jesus replied, "I say not unto thee, Until seven times: but, Until seventy times seven" (Matthew 18:22).

The lack of a forgiving spirit may not work damage and harm to the person to whom forgiveness is refused, but it surely works great harm and damage to us when we refuse to forgive. Essentially the unforgiving spirit expresses an attitude of final and just judgment as well as retribution, neither of which is appropriate for finite man since God alone is the judge of the human heart and to him alone belongs the right of retributive justice. Since all of this is true, whoever thinks he is competent to pass judgment and to exercise retributive justice falls under the judgment of God. He hurts himself more than the one against whom he has a quarrel. Such conduct betrays one's spiritual immaturity. There are Christians who will not forgive those against whom they have a grievance even though this refusal will bring themselves under the judgment of God and impose upon them needless impediments which would not be theirs if they were to forgive. This is the contrariety of human nature at work.

Scripture does not demand indiscriminate forgiveness. But even if the offenders refuse to repent we should not harbor unforgiving spirits. We cannot hate those who have hurt us, nor can we be *unwilling* to forgive them. We are always to exercise the grace of

Christian forgiveness and reconciliation when repentance occurs. Failure to forgive when repentance is evidenced is, of course, sin.

Most of us are inclined to harbor ill feelings towards those with whom we are in disagreement. We find it easier to forgive than to forget. The unwillingness to forget as well as to forgive turns out to be an unforgiving spirit. Such attitudes hinder prayer and create spiritual blocks which should be removed. Once they are removed, a new spirit of power in prayer will be felt and prayer itself will take on fresh meaning.

GENERAL HINDRANCES

There are general external physical and psychological hindrances which arrest prayer progress. Who has not been distracted by jangling telephones, raucous radios and the ever-playing TV set? Who has not found his mind wandering when on his knees in prayer? Who has not felt the lack of concentration or engaged in wool-gathering as he prayed? Who has not been at times preoccupied with other things which are good in themselves but which are foes of the best in life? Who has never been emotionally distraught, with mind and heart in turmoil, and found it impossible to pray? Who has not been overtaken by the press of other duties to the neglect of the prayer duty? Who has not been sleepy, tired or hungry, and found these problems hindering him from getting on his knees? Who has not failed to exercise personal discipline in the general matters of life and in prayer also?

We can control some of these hindrances easily. Others we cannot. We must face them matter-of-factly and deal with them one by one. Every one of them will yield if we are determined to triumph over them, but each one which remains uncontrolled will injure the life of prayer.

CONCLUSION

The hindrances we have dealt with are no more than a suggested guide. They constitute a check list against which to measure our own experiences and this enables us to determine whether our prayer problems are caused by any of these we have discussed.

Some of the items on the list will be foreign to our experience while we can surely think of others that have not been mentioned, but which trouble us. Identifying the problem is the first step toward a solution. It must be followed by a plan of action designed to overcome the problem, and the plan of action must be put into operation.

We cannot assume that we are victims of circumstances that cannot be changed. The grace of God is greater than our handicaps. However strong the shackles are that bind us they are not unbreakable. They will yield to human persistence accompanied by divine enablement. If they are not conquered we remain defeated in the life of the Spirit. But when they are acknowledged and fought against, they yield and the battle is won. We can go from grace to grace and from glory to glory in perfecting the life of prayer.

Notes

[1] *The Speaker's Bible,* The Gospel According to St. Mark, Vol. II. James Hastings, Ed. (Aberdeen: 1929), pp. 129, 130.

[2] See also additional treatment of this theme in Chapter V, "Problems in Prayer," in which the "grace of faith" and the "gift of faith" are discussed.

[3] Watt, *op. cit.,* p. 57.

VII

THE POWER OF PRAYER

In 1905 Albert Einstein developed the theory $E=mc^2$. This theory led to the development of the atom bomb. Einstein's idea, which at the time had no basis in fact, was eventually shown to work in practice. His idea became a living reality and the world has been changed immeasurably as a consequence. His theory would have remained only a theory unless and until it was tested and proved. Sometimes, however, this procedure is reversed. Long before Newton posited the law of gravity men knew that objects thrown in the air fell to the ground. This fact which all men understood was given a scientific formulation, but it remains true that if objects do not fall back to earth when thrown in the air then the theory must be changed to coincide with the facts.

The amusing story is told of how aeronautical engineers concluded that it is theoretically impossible for the lady-bug to fly. But the lady-bug knows nothing of the theory and she flies. Therefore, we must suppose there are exceptions to this law, or that the engineers lack some knowledge that would explain this exception, or their notion of the law is wrong. It is appropriate to use this methodology in connection with prayer. Theories are not facts unless they can be proved. And if the theories are not supported by the evidence, they must be scrapped.

We assert boldly that God answers prayer and that prayer

releases the mighty power of God. But if no prayers are answered and no power manifested, then the theory remains unproven or falls to the ground. But if it can be shown that prayers are answered and power manifested, then we must conclude that prayer works in practice and is more than just a theory. Certainly we must face the pragmatic test when we propound the theory that God answers prayer and ask the all-important question, "Does it really work in practice?"

Looking at the power of prayer in everyday experience in the lives of men, we ought to admit that every situation has certain unknowns in it. Therefore, if anyone asks us for incontrovertible evidence to validate the efficacy of prayer beyond all question of doubt, it is impossible to produce it. It would be equally impossible to do so in any other realm of life. But if we are willing to consider credible reports seriously and to come to conclusions based on the same kind of evidences such as we employ to arrive at conclusions in other areas of life, the power of prayer may be demonstrated to the satisfaction of reasonable men. We will not then have closed the door to all questions, nor will we have supplied final answers to every query. It does mean that the theory that prayer is an instrument of remarkable power can be established just as other accepted theses have been established in the minds of thinking men.

Reasonable men do not necessarily have to be converted men in order to understand the power of prayer. They do not need to have the same faith in God that the Christian has. Their minds do not have to be specially enlightened to spiritual truth by the Holy Spirit of God. The light afforded by general revelation, when combined with the divinely implanted rational faculties of man, is adequate to validate the thesis that God answers prayer and that prayer has power. For those of us who have been regenerated, however, the factor of faith is added. By faith our understanding is greatly enlightened and a new dimension is added to life. It is both natural and normal for Christians to believe that God releases his divine power through prayer and that prayer is the greatest latent force in the universe available to man. In the life of the unregenerate the evidence should serve to convince him that prayer is effectual. In the lives of believers it serves another purpose: it increases our faith and enables us to turn more readily and dependently to God in prayer.

If it can be shown that prayer has no power and that God does not answer prayer, then it is foolish to believe in it or practice it. If it can be demonstrated that there are no objective, external answers to prayer, or that the power of prayer is something quite different from what we claim it to be, the sooner we know this the better. We could then reappraise our opinions and adjust our theories in line with the realities of experience. Prayer cannot be divorced from human experience. Indeed all of Scripture relates it to human experience. It would have no significance if it were not so related.

This much we can say confidently. History's pages supply two kinds of evidence to support the view that prayer has power. The first comes from the testimony of countless thousands of Christians who discovered that God answered prayer and that it unloosed divine power. It is unreasonable to suppose that these people would have continued to pray fervently if they themselves never experienced any of this power in answer to their prayers. History shows that the saints of bygone years not only endorsed the theory, but also left behind them factual evidences of answered prayer which they accepted as pragmatic proof that what they believed by faith was verified in experience. Although the ordinary pages of history supply instances of this kind, we have been left with better and more reliable evidences to support our proposition. These evidences cram the pages of Scripture and are seen in the lives of ordinary men and women of like passions who believed in prayer and who experienced its power. We turn to their testimony to corroborate the thesis that God has answered prayer in the past and that the humblest saint has available to him today the mightiest power on earth.

Before examining specific examples of answered prayer in the Bible, we must understand what is meant when we say that prayer is power. This is particularly important in our age, which is acutely power conscious. Men now have at their disposal material weapons of fantastic destructive capability. Scientists claim that man's deadly power potential is so enormous that it is now possible to extinguish the entire human race on this planet. The atom bomb, the cobalt bomb, and the hydrogen bomb are among these power complexes which haunt men in this age of anxiety. To this threat must be added the terror of chemical warfare, which is equally dangerous. Along with the development of weapons of destruction science has accumulated knowledge and with it the power to work constructively. Atomic energy can change salt water into fresh. The same energy can propel vehicles through space and under water at great speeds. Rocket power and new jet engines make possible the traversal of air and space at rates of speed undreamed of a few years ago. Turbine engines drive ocean vessels of more than eighty thousand tons displacement through the water at high speed. In the realm of medicine man has discovered new means for conquering diseases that were formerly incurable. Pneumonia, smallpox, diphtheria, rabies, poliomyelitis, and numerous other diseases have yielded to the medical skills of the physician. Infant mortality has been reduced drastically and the span of life increased steadily over the years. All of these things represent power.

Against whatever standard prayer is measured, be it atomic energy, the turbine engine, medicine or the like, it possesses a latent power that equals and exceeds that devised by man or that which may ever be devised by man. All the power forms known or still to be known by men shrink into insignificance when compared to the power of prayer. And prayer carries with it a safeguard that no other power can boast of: It cannot be used successfully for evil purposes nor can it be abused to satisfy the wicked whims of men. Properly understood and faithfully used it becomes in the hands of the suppliant the most powerful force in the world. But when it is about to be misused, its power vanishes and it becomes a lifeless and valueless tool in the hands of the user. This cannot be said of any other power with which we are familiar. All other powers are subject to the will, even the caprice, of the user and thus may be employed for evil as well as for good purposes. With this by way of background, we can turn our attention to some biblical examples of the power of prayer.

ELIJAH

Elijah the Tishbite overshadows most of the Old Testament prophets. He was a man of God and a man of prayer. One of the mightiest miracles he wrought through prayer was the raising of the widow's son from the dead, a feat that no scientist can duplicate. Elijah was fed by the widow at Zarephath during a period of drought. Her son died, and, listening to the mother's appeal, Elijah carried the lad to his room and there began to wrestle mightily before God in prayer. "And he stretched himself upon the child three times, and cried unto the Lord, and said, O Lord my God, I pray thee, let this child's soul come into him again. And the Lord heard the voice of Elijah; and the soul of the child came into him again, and he revived" (1 Kings 17:21,22). Several items stand in bold outline in this prayer miracle. Elijah saw that the child was really dead. His soul had departed from his body. He prayed for the departed soul to return to its earthly tabernacle. It was Elijah's petition that God heard; it was his prayer that God answered. The reviving of the child was a demonstration of the mighty power of God.

Another incident in the life of Elijah was his encounter with the priests of Baal on Mount Carmel. One of the notable features of this confrontation was the aloneness of Elijah among all the people of Israel. There were other Israelites who had not bowed the knee to Baal; seven thousand of them were still faithful to God. But they were not in evidence here. As the sole prophet of the Lord, Elijah remained fearless in his struggle against four hundred and fifty priests of Baal (1 Kings 18:22). The true altar of God had been broken down. The people had succumbed to the deceptions of the god of Jezebel. The broken-down altar speaks all too clearly of the spiritual apostasy of Israel. Most of them had bowed the knee to Baal. Then Elijah the prophet of God began his ministry at a time when darkness prevailed throughout the land. One man, with the help of God, stood in the breach. He boldly challenged the priests of Baal to a contest of fire to determine who was the true and living God. Despite all that the advocates of Baal did, no fire came from heaven to consume their sacrifices. Even as they cut themselves until the blood flowed, Elijah mocked them. But nothing happened. To be sure, Elijah might have claimed a great victory simply because the priests of Baal got no response from their god. A man of lesser faith might then have turned aside gloating that he had won a negative victory over the priests of Baal even though no fire from heaven consumed his own sacrifice. But not Elijah.

After the priests of Baal were shown to be incapable of enlisting the help of their god, Elijah sprang into action. First he rebuilt the altar of God. Then he set the wood in order and laid the pieces of the bullock on the altar. Then, as though to mock his adversaries, he called three times for water to be poured upon the sacrifice and into the surrounding trench. At the hour of the evening sacrifice after the priests of Baal had spent their day in vain calling upon their god, Elijah went to work in prayer. It was a plain prayer that was not cluttered with useless chatter. He got to the heart of the matter speedily: "Lord God of Abraham, Isaac, and of Israel, let it be known this day that thou art God in Israel, and that I am thy servant, and that I have done all these things at thy word. Hear me, O Lord, hear me, that this people may know that thou art the Lord God, and that thou hast turned their heart back again" (1 Kings 18:36,37). Elijah knew for certain that he was in the center of the will of God. He wanted all to know that he was there in the name of the Lord God himself. Knowing this, he had great confidence as he called upon God to answer his prayer. Elijah pulled no tricks. He used no knives to cut himself. He made no spectacle by dancing and cavorting before God. His was the sublimely simple prayer of the believing heart. And the Scripture succinctly and forcefully records the result of his prayer. "Then the fire of the Lord fell" (1 Kings 18:38). The sacrifice, the wood and the water were all consumed. Even the stones and the dust disappeared. Since Elijah possessed no devices to simulate fire from heaven and could not possibly be accused of trickery, the incident demonstrates the power of prayer. The people who were present fell on their faces and said "The Lord, he is the God" (1 Kings 18:39).

Scripture affords us still another example of prayer's mighty power in the experience of Elijah. No sooner was the victory won on Carmel's heights than he informed Ahab of the sound of the abundance of rain in the face of the prolonged drought which he had previously forecast but which was now about to end. And once again he resorted to prayer as the instrument through which the prophecy of rain would be accomplished. The account in 1 Kings does not itself specifically state that Elijah prayed. It is implied, of course, in the words, "And Elijah went up to the top of Carmel; and he cast himself down upon the earth, and put his face between his knees" (1 Kings 18:42). It is later claimed by James to be prayer, when he says that Elijah "prayed again, and the heaven gave rain, and the earth brought forth her fruit" (James 5:18). Seven times the servant of Elijah went to look for rain at the command of the prophet before the answer came. Again the Scripture says very simply, "and there was a great rain." Here was God working his mighty works on behalf of a man whose knees were bent in supplication and whose heart was right.

ELISHA

If the life of Elijah offers confirming evidence that God answers prayer and that prayer has mighty power, the life and ministry of Elisha, who replaced Elijah, is no less valuable in piling up such evidences. Like his predecessor he was uniquely a man of prayer.

One answer to prayer in the life of Elisha arose out of a conversation with his servant. The question posed by the servant vividly points up the difference between him and Elisha. He walked by sight, whereas Elisha saw things through the eye of faith. The city of Dothan was compassed about by the horses and chariots of Ben-hadad, king of Syria, who had sent them to take Elisha prisoner. The servant of Elisha expressed his terror when he said, "Alas, my master! how shall we do?" (2 Kings 6:15). This was a statement of defeat. This was an acknowledgment of the seriousness of their plight. This was the counsel of despair. Elisha's answer to his servant's question contained no bitter fruit of unbelief. His was the answer of confidence and assurance. "Fear not: for they that be with us are more than they that be with them" (2 Kings 6:16). Then Elisha prayed, "Open his eyes that he may see"

(2 Kings 6:17). And when the eyes of the young man were opened he saw the mountains round about them filled with horses and chariots of fire set for the protection of the prophet of God. This was a mighty answer to prayer. The confining curtain draped about the real, but unseen, world was dropped for a moment. The young man was permitted to see behind this veil what Elisha had already seen through the eye of faith. The servant learned that there is an invisible reality which is a part of all reality and with which men must reckon. The battle is not to the strong nor the race to the swift if the counsels of God are against them. Prayer revealed this unseen power and leaves for us and our posterity the assurance that what was true in Elisha's day is true in our day too.

Elisha continued to pray asking God to blind the Syrians. And God smote the Syrians with blindness "according to the word of Elisha" (2 Kings 6:18). Elisha then led the blinded Syrians to Samaria. Upon their arrival he asked God to restore their sight and again his prayer was answered. On the surface these answers to prayer may seem to have been capricious. But when viewed against the background of the national political situation they were acts of mighty deliverance. Elisha did not lead the Syrians to Samaria for them to be murdered. When they arrived he convinced the king of Israel that they should not be slaughtered. In effect, Elisha asked why the king should slay soldiers who had been delivered into his hand without his having to fight, when normally he would not have slain captives taken in actual armed combat. Elisha advised the king of Israel to feed them and to treat them well. This in turn brought national deliverance because "the bands of Syria came no more into the land of Israel" (2 Kings 6:23). Such were the effects wrought by the prayers of Elisha, the prophet of God.

MOSES

Moses the great deliverer was also Moses the man of prayer. His years were filled with difficult circumstances that drove him to God in prayer. His life by itself supplies sufficient proofs of the power of God through prayer to silence the arguments of the most pronounced sceptic. The prayers of Moses are of special value because they encompass so much territory. The very diversity of the circumstances and the variety of his requests spell out the uniqueness of his prayer life. Of all the prayers he made, none reaches higher than his simple request to God when he said, "I beseech thee, shew me thy glory" (Exodus 33:18). No man may see God in his essence and live, yet God made it possible for Moses to experience what the eyes of mortal men have never known. He hid Moses in the cleft of a rock and passed by. And when the presence of God had passed by, Moses was permitted to see his "back parts" (Exodus 33:23) the sight of which was more than sufficient to satisfy the deepest longing of his heart. Here was the self revelation of God to a mere mortal, given in answer to a simple but effective prayer.

During the wilderness wandering the children of Israel became chronic complainers. In one instance their complaints brought divine judgment in the form of fire which consumed many of them at Taberah. In their distress the people turned to Moses who, in turn, prayed to God for mercy. As a result of his prayer the "fire was quenched" (Numbers 11:2). Later the Israelites murmured against God again. Fiery serpents were sent in judgment upon the people because of this sin. Once again the people pleaded with Moses to seek the face of God to stop the judgment. Scripture says that "Moses prayed for the people" (Numbers 21:7). We see here intercession at its best. Here was one whose concern for others made him bow his knee to the God of heaven on their behalf. In response to Moses' prayer God commanded him to make a brazen serpent. Anyone who was bitten by one of the fiery serpents needed only to look upon the brazen serpent which was held aloft, and whoever looked, lived. From this incident comes the far more remarkable and miraculous fulfilment in the New Testament. The brazen serpent is a type of Christ. As Moses lifted up the brazen serpent and those who looked escaped the penalty of their sins, so Jesus Christ has been lifted up for the sins of men. Whoever looks upon him in faith is delivered from the penalty and the guilt of his sins. The actual historical incident to which John made reference in his Gospel is a remarkable answer to a prayer offered by Moses, the intercessor. The delivering and saving power of God displayed in answer to Moses' many prayers, of which we have given only a sample, cannot be gainsaid. They ever remain as a shining testimony to the power of God that is released in answer to prayer.

SAMUEL

Samuel, the prophet of God, was the product of prayer. His mother, Hannah, prayed for a man child and God heard her prayer. Samuel was the answer to this prayer. His parents devoted him to God from his birth. He served under Eli and replaced him when he died. Samuel enjoyed two distinct benefits in his early years: he was reared by parents who knew the power of God in response to prayer; and he served under Eli who also was familiar with the power of prayer. During Samuel's day the Israelites suffered greatly from the depredations of the Philistines. They looked to Samuel for help in their distress. He told them to put away their strange gods and to serve the Lord. He also instructed them to "gather all Israel to Mizpeh, and I will *pray* for you unto the Lord" (1 Samuel 7:5). The people themselves urged Samuel, "Cease not to cry unto the Lord our God for us, that he will save us out of the hand of the Philistines" (1 Samuel 7:8). We are then told that "Samuel cried unto the Lord for Israel; and the Lord heard him" (1 Samuel 7:9). In response to Samuel's prayer the Lord "thundered with a great thunder on that day upon the Philistines, and discomfited them; and they were smitten before Israel" (1 Samuel 7:10). Samuel then set up a stone and named it Ebenezer (hitherto the Lord hath helped us). The results of his prayer and God's answer were so great that "the Philistines were subdued, and they came no more into the coast of Israel: and the hand of the Lord was against the Philistines all the days of Samuel" (1 Samuel 7:13).

Samuel's prayers for deliverance from the Philistines were certainly not personal prayers for his immediate benefit. They were national requests prayed for the entire people of Israel in times of political and military crisis. God intervened on behalf of his people because of Samuel's prayers. The truth which emerges from this

and other prayers for national deliverance in trying times is that
the cynical statement of Napoleon that God is always on the side
of the last reserve is not true. Over and over again Israel saw God's
mighty power unleashed for them when outward circumstances
made any hope of military victory against their enemies a virtual
impossibility. This claim may be corroborated by recalling incidents which have been mentioned previously. Jehoshaphat (2
Chronicles 20) saw God's power manifested when his people were
delivered from the armies of the children of Ammon, Moab and
Mount Seir. Hezekiah (2 Kings 19:14 ff) saw that same power
employed when he and his people were freed from the menace of
the Assyrians under Sennacherib, their mighty monarch. And the
God of Samuel, Jehoshaphat and Hezekiah is not dead today. He
still sits in the heavens and laughs at those who make light of this
mighty power. He still waits for nations to put their trust in him for
deliverance from those who are his enemies. One need only read
the accounts of the invasion of the mainland of Europe by the
Allied troops who fought against Hitler, to see the principle of
God's power demonstrated in modern history. The fantastic number of blunders committed by the Nazi high command, Adolph
Hitler himself, and the Luftwaffe, cannot be explained logically.
There were simply too many of them. These blunders insured the
success of the beachhead and finally resulted in the downfall of the
fascist dictators. The hand of God was at work, and it is not
difficult for Christians to see God in this, remembering that millions of believers were praying for the defeat of these God-defying
men of wickedness. It is also well to note then, that military might
is not sufficient in itself. Men and nations still must look to the
power of God and his intervening grace in history.

THE MAN OF GOD AND JEROBOAM

An unnamed prophet of God came face to face with King
Jeroboam of Israel in the midst of his wickedness. He spoke to
Jeroboam concerning the altar he had built at Bethel, prophesying
that it would be rent asunder and the ashes upon it poured out. An
enraged Jeroboam sought to lay hold of the prophet. As he
reached forth his hand to do so his hand "dried up, so that he

could not pull it in again to him" (1 Kings 13:4). Then Jeroboam pleaded with the man of God, "Intreat now the face of the Lord thy God, and pray for me, that my hand may be restored me again. And the man of God besought the Lord, and the king's hand was restored him again, and became as it was before" (v.6).

This was an unusual incident. It illustrates first the immediate and intervening power of God on behalf of his servant when Jeroboam would have slain him. But it also reveals the operation of the direct power of God to reverse the situation in response to the prayer of the prophet. God does touch bodies through prayer, and healing does occur immediately by the power of God as well as through secondary means and agencies.

MANASSEH

Hezekiah was sick unto death. He prayed to God asking for an extension of life. He was granted another fifteen years in answer to prayer. During this period his son Manasseh was born. He ascended to his father's throne when he was only twelve years of age, and reigned fifty-five years, doing evil in the sight of the Lord. Yet Manasseh received an answer to prayer which manifested the power of God and demonstrates the common mercy of God even to one who walked in wickedness. The Assyrians took Manesseh captive and carried him bound to Babylon. In the midst of this ignominy and disgrace the Scripture says, "He besought the Lord his God, and humbled himself greatly before the God of his fathers, and prayed unto him" (2 Chronicles 33:12,13). God "heard his supplication, and brought him again to Jerusalem into his kingdom" (2 Chronicles 33:13). This mighty answer convinced him that the Lord was God, and he mended his ways. The account closes with an observation about Manasseh's prayer, revealing how unusual the incident must have been. The summary states that "the rest of the acts of Manasseh, and his prayer unto his God . . . are written in the book of the kings of Israel" (2 Chronicles 33:18). Its importance is then reiterated by the words "his prayer also, and how God was intreated of him, . . . are written among the sayings of the seers" (2 Chronicles 33:19). While the record does not afford very much information concern-

ing the captivity and release of Manasseh, the episodes must have
been extraordinary ones for them to be mentioned both in the
book of the kings of Israel and in the sayings of the seers.

JEREMIAH

The "weeping prophet" Jeremiah sought God's help in prayer
on many occasions. And God spoke to him many times concerning
the plight of the people. One of the most enthralling of Jeremiah's
prayers sprang out of a request by the people of the land, the
captains of the forces, and leading individuals. They asked him to
pray to God and seek the divine will. Jeremiah promised, "I will
pray unto the Lord your God according to your words; and it shall
come to pass, that whatsoever thing the Lord shall answer you, I
will declare it unto you" (Jeremiah 42:4). Jeremiah's prayer was
answered by God as Jeremiah himself attested: "Thus saith the
Lord, the God of Israel, unto whom ye sent me to present your
supplication before him" (Jeremiah 42:9). God's answer to Jeremiah's prayer was singularly difficult for the people to accept. They
thought that national safety and deliverance from the power of
Babylon were to be found by fleeing to Egypt. God told Jeremiah
to command them to remain in their own land, and God promised
that he would deliver them there by his mighty power. They were
also told that if they did flee to Egypt they would die by the sword,
by famine and by pestilence. Here was a sure word from God in
answer to prayer. Whichever way the people took, the mighty
power of God would be perceptible. If they remained in the land
they would see his mighty delivering power; if they went to Egypt
they would see his mighty devouring power. Deliverance was
promised if they obeyed him; defeat and destruction were threatened if they disobeyed. The people foolishly decided that Jeremiah's prayer had not be answered by God and that the word he
brought was a false and not a true word from the Lord. They lived
to regret their decision, for they then experienced the power of an
avenging and destroying God rather than his delivering mercies.

DANIEL

One of Daniel's prayers opens still another kind of window for
us to observe how available God's power is to those who are

faithful in their prayer lives. The account in question turns around the incident in which Daniel was cast into the lion's den. The record does not say that Daniel prayed when he was thrown to the lions. We can suppose that he did pray, but this cannot be stated dogmatically. Yet Daniel was the type of person who in such a critical experience of life would have sought the face of God, and we may properly conclude that he did. But even if Daniel did not resort to prayer at the time he was thrown into the lions' den, the Scripture does indicate that those who are faithful in prayer as a rule and practice of life will not be deserted by God when their very practice of prayer produces persecution and punishment. Darius issued a proclamation forbidding all men from making petitions to any god or man except himself for a period of thirty days. Daniel encountered a serious problem because it was his custom to seek the face of God three times a day. He did not cease his habit of prayer when the prohibition was issued. ". . . he kneeled upon his knees three times a day, and prayed, and gave thanks before his God, as he did aforetime" (Daniel 6:10). Darius was not personally disposed to throw Daniel to the lions for his breach of the law, but he had bound himself irrevocably when he issued his decree. Therefore, he kept his word and Daniel became the victim of his enemies' cleverness. Daniel's foes had not reckoned on the power of God by which he shut the mouths of the lions so that Daniel was not consumed. This was a miraculous act. Its effect was heightened when Darius cast the enemies of Daniel to the same lions who then mastered them and killed them and their families. We must take seriously the contrast which the story makes evident. There is no explanation for the deliverance of Daniel and the death of his persecutors apart from the mighty power of a prayer-answering God.

We have every right to expect God to do great things for us if we are regular and faithful in our praying. Indeed it is an encouragement to all of God's faithful people to know that prayer warriors can expect God to help them in circumstances when they cannot pray. God, who searches the heart, knows that they would have moved heaven and earth with their prayers had there been time. When the attitude and the intention of the heart is right it avails for those who truly love God.

JONAH

Jonah, God's wayward prophet, has left us with another sample of power through prayer. God summoned him to call the people of Nineveh to repentance. Instead of doing what he was told he bought a ticket on a ship to sail for Tarshish to escape from the presence of the Lord and thus leave Nineveh to perish because of its sins. Since Tarshish was probably located in Spain, it is apparent that Jonah intended to flee as far from God as it was possible to go in those days. He quickly found out what so many others have learned the hard way—that God will not overlook disobedience, and that man cannot flee from his presence. When Jonah was thrown overboard and landed in the belly of the great fish he had ample time to meditate. He repented of his foolish act of fleeing from God and turned to him in prayer, seeking forgiveness. His prayer (Jonah 2) might well be used as a model by all who fall into the sin of disobedience. It was an effective prayer, for the fish promptly turned toward the shore and literally spewed Jonah out of its mouth onto the dry land. This was a mighty act of God; it was a divine deliverance and it has been recorded for our benefit. What God was in Jonah's day, God is today.

ZACHARIAS

Zacharias was the father of John the Baptist. The story of John's birth is a chronicle of perseverance in prayer resulting in a remarkable exhibition of God's might. The predicament of Zacharias and Elizabeth his wife is stated by Luke who says, "they had no child, because that Elizabeth was barren, and they both were now well stricken in years" (Luke 1:7). Zacharias was engaged in the duties of his priestly office. As he burned incense an angel of the Lord appeared to him. He was troubled and fear came upon him. The angel said to him, "Thy prayer is heard" (Luke 1:13). Zacharias was a knowledgeable person; the first thought that arose in his mind was that his wife could not possibly give birth to a child. He asked the key question, not only out of incredulity, but out of awe and wonder: "Whereby shall I know this? for I am an old man, and my wife well stricken in years" (Luke 1:18). The angel replied that he was Gabriel who had come from the presence of God. He had been sent to reveal this promise to Zacharias. He said, "Behold, thou shalt be dumb, and not able to speak, until the day that these things shall be performed, because thou believest not my words, which shall be fulfilled in their season" (Luke 1:20).

The prayers of Zacharias and Elizabeth for a child had been prayed over a long period of time. The delayed answer undoubtedly led them to conclude that there was no hope of an affirmative response. The biological factors were reasonable grounds for them to conclude that their prayers would not be answered as they hoped. But the power of God is not limited by the biological details of life. He still is the God of the impossible. He does do things that run counter to the commonly accepted laws of nature. Miracles, while they occur infrequently, are still included in the plan of God who answers prayer. Perhaps the most telling statement made in conjunction with this unusual answer to prayer came when John was born. The relatives and neighbors of Elizabeth "heard how the Lord had shewed great mercy upon her; and they rejoiced with her" (Luke 1:58).

PENTECOST

The experience of Jesus' disciples at Pentecost is inseparably tied to prayer. Jesus himself commanded them to tarry in Jerusalem until they were endued with power from on high (Luke 24:49). As they tarried, they prayed. They looked for the promised Spirit. Luke says, "These all continued with one accord in prayer and supplication, with the women, and Mary the mother of Jesus, and with his brethren" (Acts 1:14). On the day of Pentecost "they were all with one accord in one place" (Acts 2:1). It is important to note that the promise of the Spirit's coming is mentioned several times. We cannot conclude that the Spirit would not have come even if the followers of Jesus had failed to pray. But God ordains the secondary means as well as the ends, and prayer was definitely a part of the secondary means in the pentecostal experience. Through prayer the disciples of Jesus were prepared for the coming of the Holy Spirit. Their hearts were made ready.

At Pentecost at least two extraordinary events took place. First, there was the twofold physical phenomena: the sound from heaven like a mighty rushing wind which filled the whole house where the disciples were gathered, and the cloven tongues like as of fire which sat upon each one of those assembled. Then there was the gift of tongues in which the disciples spoke the languages of those who were assembled in Jerusalem for the celebration of Pentecost. Specific tongues are not mentioned. Rather geographical areas are listed and in all probability there were more tongues spoken than geographical areas listed. The remarkable phenomenon of the gift of tongues greatly affected those who listened to the disciples speak in their own languages. They knew that the disciples were not able to speak these tongues normally. Moreover they knew that even if the disciples were able to speak different languages they would not have been able to speak them perfectly. It was with amazement that the listeners heard their own tongues spoken so well. Some suggested that the followers of Jesus were full of new wine; in short, they were drunk. It was Peter who supplied the biblical interpretation of this event. His explanation was simple to the point of absurdity. God had poured out his Spirit upon all flesh. And this outpouring was preceded by ten days of uninterrupted prayer in which the disciples were of one mind or of one accord. Thus prayer, the power of God, and Pentecost are locked together to form one frame of reference, and again we see the power generated by prayer.

THE EARLY CHURCH

The coming of the Holy Spirit at Pentecost was not the end but the beginning of new things. Literally thousands of people were converted. The conversion of these multitudes led to persecution by those who opposed the new faith. Peter and John, who were in the leadership of the revival movement, were forbidden to preach in the name of Jesus. The miracle of Pentecost, which the enemies of the church recognized as such, had caused a great stir. The further miracle of the healing of the lame man at the temple gate aroused admiration in some and opposition in others. The entrenched religious leaders feared for their ecclesiastical futures.

The new thrust and the mighty power of the disciples of Jesus seemed to strike at their authority, their prestige, and their religious hold on the people. They could have joined the disciples and furthered the cause of Christ. Instead they threatened them and forbade them to preach in the name of Jesus. The disciples understood clearly how dangerous this made their situation. These enemies were the ones who had crucified the Lord of glory. They would not refrain from doing the same to the followers of their victim.

The reaction of Peter and John to persecution was typical. They went back to their brethren and employed their greatest resource against persecution—prayer. Acts 4 is the story of this persecution and of the prayer meeting which followed. The consequences of the prayer meeting are illuminating and astonishing. Once again they were filled with the Holy Spirit; the place where they were staying was shaken; once again they spoke the word of God with boldness. The Scripture indicates that other results occurred. The disciples "were of one heart and of one soul," "with great power gave the apostles witness of the resurrection of the Lord Jesus," "great grace was upon them all," "neither was there any among them that lacked . . . and distribution was made unto every man according as he had need" (Acts 4:31–37).

It would be imprudent to suggest that this kind of apostolic experience is a necessary norm or that it should be repeated in our day. Historical circumstances differ from age to age, but God does not change. He does not work the same way in every age, although he does work according to times and circumstances. But the principle remains. There is, therefore, no reason why the church cannot see similar remarkable responses to its prayers. God is the same yesterday, today, and forever.

THE APOSTLE PETER

Peter was a man of many weaknesses. Yet he had at least one strength. He knew when and how to pray. While the prayers of Peter recorded in the Bible do not equal in number those of Jesus or of Paul, nonetheless they represent a strong link in the chain of proof which demonstrates the power of prayer.

Peter had no power within himself to raise the dead. But he was able to pray and through prayer God raised the dead. The case of Tabitha attests to this. She was a devout, god-fearing woman full of good works. She became sick, died, and was prepared for burial. The disciples heard that Peter was in the area and two of the brethren appealed to him for help. Peter returned with them and entered into the room where the body of Tabitha lay. He sent out the mourners and then "he kneeled down, and prayed" (Acts 9:40). When he had done this he addressed the lifeless body saying, "Tabitha, arise. And she opened her eyes: and when she saw Peter, she sat up." This certainly was a stupendous feat. The dead had been raised. But a still greater miracle arose out of the incident. When the news of Tabitha's resurrection was noised abroad "many believed in the Lord" (Acts 9:42). The greater miracle of conversion and regeneration was the outgrowth of the raising of Tabitha from the dead. And it all had its origin in the prayer of Peter.

Another incident in the life of Peter was his release from jail, which was the direct result of prayer. Undoubtedly he prayed for himself. But the church also prayed for him without ceasing. The results of these prayers were extraordinary. An angel came to Peter in prison. The chains fell off his hands and the iron gate opened of its own accord. And when Peter arrived at the home of Mary he found his friends praying for him. However one may try to account for Peter's release as a coincidence, accident or happenstance, the number of odd circumstances surrounding his release make this impossible. The only plausible explanation is that God, in answer to prayer, intervened supernaturally and delivered Peter. Thus was God's power seen in response to believing prayer.

In another case, God used Peter as an instrument in the conversion of Cornelius. He was not exactly an enthusiastic witness since Cornelius was a Gentile and Peter was not yet convinced that the Gospel really was for the Gentiles. At about the sixth hour, Peter went up to the housetop to pray. During his prayer time God spoke to him through a vision. Peter learned that God wanted him to go to Cornelius with the word of salvation. It was this vision, coming in the hour of prayer, that opened the gates of the kingdom to the Gentiles and made it plain that God is no respecter of persons.

One of the important prayers in the life of Peter was the one prayed by the Lord Jesus himself. After the Last Supper had been instituted Jesus spoke to his disciples of the fate that awaited him in Jerusalem. He predicted that Peter would deny him and then told him, "Satan hath desired to have you, that he may sift you as wheat: But I have prayed for thee, that thy faith fail not: and when thou art converted, strengthen thy brethren. (Luke 22:31,32). This prayer of Jesus was abundantly answered. With the coming of the Holy Spirit at Pentecost Peter was strengthened. He became a vocal and radiant witness of Jesus Christ. He preached one sermon which brought three thousand souls into the kingdom of God. Great grace came upon him; fearlessness instead of fearfulness became his watchword; strength instead of weakness characterized his life. He was a truly transformed man and all of this occurred because Christ prayed for him. Beyond any doubt the closing years of Peter's life overshadowed his earlier years and this took place in answer to the prayer of Jesus through which the power of his Father was made available in transforming his servant.

THE APOSTLE PAUL

Paul is best known for his missionary activities. If we reconsider his life we will surely place more emphasis on his prayers for they were even more important than his missionary work. Next to Jesus there is no one in the New Testament about whom more has been written concerning prayer than the Apostle Paul. It was Paul who commanded us to pray without ceasing. It was Paul who wrote to various churches claiming that he had not ceased to pray for them. It was Paul who practiced what he preached and made prayer central in his own life and walk. It was Paul who left us this rich legacy and convinces us today that there is power in prayer. The centrality of prayer in the life of Paul may be seen from the fact that he began his Christian life steeped in prayer. After he had been blinded on the Damascus Road when he saw the risen Christ, he was led to the home of Judas who lived on Straight Street in

Damascus. Ananias was sent to speak to Paul and to restore his sight to him. It was the Lord who said to Ananias that when he arrived at Judas' house he would find that "he (Paul) prayeth" (Acts 9:11). Who can deny that Paul's eyes were opened and his sight restored through the power of prayer?

God used Paul as the human instrument in the conversion of the Philippian jailor. But the conversion occurred in conjunction with the miracles of physical deliverance that came to Paul and Silas as a result of their midnight prayers. They had been imprisoned in the first place because of an incident that had to do with faithful prayer. A certain girl was possessed of a spirit of divination. She met Paul and Silas as they went to pray. Paul adjured the evil spirit to come out of her. Her masters' financial loss, due to her deliverance, led to the imprisonment of Paul and Silas. They were beaten and their feet put in stocks. At midnight they began to praise God and to pray. The prisoners, as well as God, heard them pray. The place was shaken by a great earthquake. The doors of the prison were opened. The shackles that bound the prisoners were loosed. The keeper, fearing that the prisoners had escaped and that his life would be forfeited, was about to commit suicide. He was stopped by Paul who then had the privilege of presenting Jesus Christ to him (Acts 16). Thus was the power of God seen through prayer.

It was in prayer that Paul learned the will of God. He so testified before the multitudes as he recounted the working of God's power in his own life. He stated that he had been praying in the temple. He went into a trance, in which he saw the Lord who commanded him to leave Jerusalem in haste. He did so and his life evidently was spared as a consequence of his obedience. And his obedience was a direct result of guidance received when he was in prayer (see Acts 22:17 ff.).

During the last years of his life Paul was shipped off to Rome as a prisoner for the sake of Jesus Christ. He was sent there for his case to be heard by Caesar since he had appealed to the emperor. This was his right and privilege as a Roman citizen. En route, the ship on which Paul sailed was overtaken by a bad storm. The ship was wrecked and the people aboard were stranded on what is now known as the island of Malta. No life was lost in the shipwreck, even as Paul had prophesied. He claimed that God had revealed to him that the ship would sink but that every life would be saved.

On the island, Paul was bitten by a viper. The people expected him to die, but no harm came to him. This caused them to say that he was a god (Acts 28:6). The chief man of the island was a certain Publius who housed the shipwrecked people, at least Paul and his Roman guards. The father of Publius "lay sick of a fever and of a bloody flux." Paul entered into his sickroom and prayed for him. He laid hands upon him and he was healed. Immediately other sick people on the island came to Paul and they were also healed. The Scripture does not say that Paul simply healed them without resort to prayer. He prayed, and then healing came. In accord with the facts it is perfectly proper to claim that the healings were a direct result of prayer. It was simply another instance of the mighty power of God unleashed through the means of prayer which God has ordained to secure mighty things from him.

The Scriptures proclaim that the "wonders" in the Word of God have been written for our admonition, counsel, help, and encouragement. Moreover, God is no less God today, and he continues to do great and marvelous things. This does not mean, however, that all of our prayers will be answered in the affirmative and that God will never deny us what we ask. Paul was beaten, shipwrecked, imprisoned, let down over the city wall in a basket, and exposed to a hundred other indignities.

As a man of prayer Paul may have prayed to be kept from these sufferings just as he prayed for deliverance from the thorn in the flesh. But as God did not choose to remove that thorn, so God allowed these other events to take place in his life despite his fervent prayers for divine deliverance. This dichotomy exists and the mystery which it produces cannot be fully fathomed, no matter how hard we strive to pierce through the shadows. Yet the truth ever remains that God does do mighty things in answer to prayer. And the experiences of others serve to convince us that this is so. From them we gain courage and strength to experience for ourselves similar wonderful responses to prayer.

THE LORD JESUS

The life of Jesus is the prototype of what our lives should be. A discussion of prayer would be incomplete without an examination of Jesus' own experiences in prayer. His life unveils to us the unique example of the potential and the possibilities that lie in prayer. None of us can mirror his life perfectly because of our imperfect natures. This knowledge leads to humility just as it becomes a cause for hope and rejoicing. We need not be downcast because we cannot attain to Christ's perfection. Rather we ought to rejoice in the measure to which we approximate that perfection, and we can strive to realize it more and more each day.

The prayer life of Jesus Christ takes us far beyond the examples set by the prophets and the apostles. He brings us a new appreciation of the possibilities of prayer and opens up dimensions that would otherwise remain closed. His prayers run the full gamut of human experience and fit into, and illustrate, prayer in almost every conceivable category. Our concern here is not to delve into the richness of Jesus' prayer life but through it to validate the claim that prayer is power, the greatest power to be found on earth. And that it is a power that is available to the humblest child and the greatest saint. How, then, does the prayer life of Jesus manifest the mighty power of his Father?

The life of Jesus is more than just a model held before us to demonstrate his uniqueness. Rather his life teaches us lasting lessons, and leaves us with certain incontrovertible facts. The Gospel writers eloquently testify that Jesus made much use of prayer in his own life. Thus it is stated, ". . . he went out into a mountain to pray, and continued all night in prayer to God" (Luke 6:12). In Luke 5:16 it is reported that "he withdrew himself into the wilderness, and prayed." In Mark 6:46 the record says that "when he had sent them away, he departed into a mountain to pray." Luke 9:28 says "It came to pass about an eight days after these sayings, he took Peter and John and James, and went up into a mountain to pray." Surely no passage of Scripture speaks more eloquently about Jesus' prayer life than does John 17. No other intercessory prayer in Scripture equals it. Here is communion with the Father at its best. From this and from the other accounts we can draw some profitable conclusions.

If Jesus is God, as the Scriptures teach, and if he is also true man, as the Scriptures also teach, then it follows that as true man he needed to be in contact with his Father. If the true man, who lived in sinless life, needed to have this prayer fellowship then sinful men are even more in need of this kind of communion. Therefore, if Jesus prayed it is necessary for everyone else to pray. And however much he needed prayer, as to time and effort spent in its exercise, his followers need it even more than he did. So the people of God should make prayer as central to their lives as Jesus made it to his.

There is more to the example of Jesus than this. What he *did* as *man* was related to *how* he prayed as *man*. The power that was given him from his Father was granted to one who had become flesh and dwelt among us. It was given to the one who "emptied himself" and took upon him the form of a servant and was made after the likeness of sinful flesh. Yet this one who was made like his brothers in the flesh displayed a power in his life so notable that it jolts the imagination. Jesus performed daring exploits as man. If the followers of Jesus are to do great exploits for God they must mirror the pattern disclosed in the life of Jesus, and that pattern has prayer for a central motif. This will stand out compellingly as we examine some of the answers Jesus received to his prayers.

Jesus took Peter, James and John into a mountain to pray. This mount of transfiguration incident is recorded in the synoptic gospels. While Jesus was busy at prayer a unique change occurred: "The fashion of his countenance was altered" (Luke 9:29). Jesus was transformed. The Greek word used of this change in Mark 9:2 and Matthew 17:2 is the one from which we derive the English word "metamorphosed." This word has in it the idea of "change of form, structure, or substance . . . the form resulting from metamorphosis." Luke no doubt was equally familiar with this particular word but he refrained from using it. In a down to earth way Luke said "The appearance of his face became different." At any rate the records of the event indicate plainly that the prayer of Jesus wrought a great outward change in him and his glory was unveiled for his disciples to see. Even his clothing was affected. It became "white gleaming."

In addition to the change that took place in Jesus on the mount of transfiguration, Moses and Elijah appeared on the scene. They were manifested "in glory" and talked with Jesus. The sleeping disciples, who had failed to maintain a prayer vigil with the Lord Jesus, were awakened. They were agitated. Peter haphazardly suggested that they erect three tabernacles in honor of the three persons present, but he did not understand what he was saying. He was equally baffled by the uncommon phenomena. Then a cloud enveloped them and when it had passed by, the disciples were alone with Jesus whose face and garments had returned to their normal condition. What cannot be overlooked as we gaze with amazement at these miraculous and soul-shaking incidents is the fact that they occurred while Jesus was engaged in prayer. It was then that the power of God was displayed in an extraordinary fashion.

A second prayer-power happening in the life of Jesus transpired in the Garden of Gethsemane. Matthew quotes Jesus as saying: "My soul is exceeding sorrowful, even unto death" (Matthew 26:38). Mark says Jesus was "sore amazed" and "very heavy" (Mark 14:33). Luke the physician notes Jesus as "being in an agony . . . and his sweat was as it were great drops of blood falling down to the ground" (Luke 22:44). Three times Jesus prayed for the cup to pass from his lips. Each time he attached a qualification to his prayer—"Not my will, but thine, be done."

Various scholars have interpreted this prayer of Jesus differently. Some think that he successfully fought a mighty battle against Satan who sought to kill him before he could go to the cross. In this case his prayer was answered affirmatively and he was strengthened and delivered so that he could go on to Calvary. The other view is that Jesus, in his humanity, prayed that if there were some other way for redemption to be wrought than by the way of the cross, God would let that way prevail. He prayed this prayer in grueling agony because he knew what going to Calvary entailed and he shrank from it. His prayer was answered. God said that there was no other way than the way of Calvary. Jesus' real prayer was to do the will of his Father, and the will of the Father prevailed. Jesus willingly left Gethsemane to go to Calvary.

We cannot read the gospel records of this dramatic episode without being struck by the difference between the Jesus on his knees in agony sweating as it were great drops of blood, and the Jesus who strode out to meet those who had come to take him captive. Rising from his knees he told his sleeping disciples that his hour had come. As they went out from the garden to face the soldiers and Judas Iscariot, Jesus shows no signs of panic. He is calm and controlled. He is the master of the situation. His enemies are the ones who fall back in dismay and disarray. Jesus is triumphant. However we may interpret the Garden of Gethsemane incident, this much is clear. The prayer of Jesus prevailed. The Father gave him all the power he needed in preparation for the climactic act of his life. There is a sense in which Gethsemane overarched the closing events of Jesus' life. It was here that a crowning victory was won. And this victory was the product of Jesus' prayer.

The supreme prayer-power incident in the life of Jesus happened at his crucifixion. Seven times he spoke from the cross. Some of these utterances were prayers. Others had to do with various matters such as commending his mother to the care of his disciple, the simple observation, "I thirst," and the promise to the dying thief that he would be with him in Paradise. Among the prayers offered by Jesus while on the cross was one having to do with the power of his Father in relation to prayer. This prayer is recorded by Luke who quotes Jesus as saying, "Father, into thy hands I commend my spirit" (Luke 23:46). When Jesus had finished praying this prayer he gave up his spirit, or surrendered his life as a sacrifice unto death. The event demonstrates the magnitude of the power that can be harnessed through prayer.

When Jesus commended his spirit to his Father and gave up the ghost he did so of his own free will. He did it knowing that two salutary effects would flow from this voluntary sacrifice. First, it would make possible the forgiveness of sins. Atonement would be made; God would be propitiated. The gates of heaven would be opened to sinners through faith in Christ and his atoning merit.

The second effect of his death was his resurrection from the dead. Were he to remain in bondage to death then Satan would triumph, not Jesus. If he did not rise, the purpose of his incarnation would have been in vain. A dead Christ could not be a saving Christ. And to continue under the state of death would nullify the intention of his prayer when he surrendered his spirit to his Father and gave up his life as a ransom. Thus the prayer of Jesus was the one that evinced the power of God in two ways. First, God accepted the atonement of Jesus and freed sinners from the guilt and the penalty of their sins. Secondly, the Father raised the Son from the dead. The prayer of Jesus included both of these things and had either of them failed to take place, then the prayer of Jesus would have been ineffectual. But both results took place. The forgiveness of sins and the resurrection of the dead, two of the greatest wonders known to men, effectively demonstrated that the power of God had been released through the prayer of Jesus as he hung on the cross. These two fruits of Jesus' mediatorial work are at the heart of the gospel. Without them there would be no gospel. With them we have the gospel, and along with this gospel we see the power of the Father manifested in response to the prayer of the Son.

CONCLUSION

The questions we asked at the beginning of this chapter have been answered. Prayer is more than a theory; it is more than a mental exercise. When used properly it changes one's thinking and alters one's orientation. Events and circumstances are affected too. In sum, prayer accomplishes what is, humanly speaking, impossible.

Once we accept the Bible as a source book, take it with great earnestness, and regard it as historical rather than legendary, then prayer becomes a real and dynamic factor in life. The men and women of the Bible were true human beings who everywhere prayed with the conviction that God would hear and answer them. Answered prayer was their commonplace experience and confirmed their deepest belief that prayer is power. The pragmatic test of everyday workability demonstrated to them indubitably that prayer is a living reality, not just a theoretical principle. Prudent and reasonable men, noting what transpired in their lives, willingly acknowledge that prayer is not some esoteric, nebulous fancy of neurotic people. They are compelled to admit that it is a true part of the structure of reality and actually works for believing men and women as they walk, sometimes painfully, sometimes blissfully, but always prayerfully through this pilgrim journey.

We may be assured that if prayer was an effective instrument in the lives of people like Moses, Abraham, Elijah, Elisha, Isaiah, Jeremiah, John, Paul, Peter and Jesus, it can and should be an equally useful instrument in the lives of Johnny Jones, Sammy Smith and Mary Johnson in contemporary life. What God has done for others through prayer he can and will do for us now, and for generations of men yet unborn. The only limitations placed upon the power of God which is released through prayer are those which he has set and the safeguards with which he has surrounded it. For all time it will ever remain the greatest force in the world and men have yet to see all that God can do through prayer. It has no substitute, accepts no counterfeit, and in its pure and unalloyed state it opens the door to a garden of beauty, a house of joy, a room of peace, a throne of grace, and the heart of God.

VIII

ILLUSTRATIONS OF ANSWERED PRAYER

We have talked of the power of prayer and we have listened to the assurances from God in Scripture that he answers prayer. Is this sufficient? The answer is obvious. No! If the Scriptures promise that God will save men in Jesus Christ and no one gets saved, then of what value is the promise that men will be saved? If the Bible supplies many illustrations of answered prayer and if it promises that God will hear and answer prayer today but no prayers outside of Scripture have been heard and answered then all of Scripture's promises mean nothing.

Men have been saved and lives have been transformed through the centuries. The books of history are filled with convincing illustrations of this tremendous fact. It is equally true that we do not need to read much or search long before we discover a wealth of material showing that countless thousands of men and women have prayed and their prayers have been answered. So great is the historical testimony to answered prayer that to deny the evidences would manifest incredible blindness on the part of the observer, or it would demonstrate the acceptance of presuppositions by the observer that he would not relinquish even though the mass of data would satisfy any objective jury in the land.

All efforts to deny the evidences that God still answers prayer must fall to the ground. To claim that all of the testimony is false will not do. To say that multiplied millions of people have been deceived is the height of folly. To argue that these people have been psychologized or manipulated would simply falsify all reality and leave all men stranded in a morass of quicksand about anything and everything. At this point we Christians who believe that God answers prayer are fairer to the evidences than those who deny it.

We readily concede that some events occur that cannot be accounted for by natural explanations. We acknowledge that some of these phenomena are to be found among those who do not profess Christianity, indeed who adhere to religions that are antithetical to Christianity. But we do not say that such unusual events cannot take place. Rather we admit their occurrence and attribute them to demonic forces that have power to counterfeit miracles, and to their leader the Devil himself, the prince of this world, who appears at times as though he were an angel of light but who cannot succeed in deceiving those who trust in Jesus Christ.

We also recognize that at times it may be difficult to discern whether something comes from the hand of God or the hand of Satan. Since we cannot fathom the human heart and cannot always know whether men who pray and ask for outside help are true or false believers, it may be that we attribute to God some things that are not his work at all, although he permits them to happen. We who believe are not disturbed by this cosmic conflict between God and Satan, nor do we see anything strange in the fact that Satan has power to imitate some of the acts of God. Indeed, on occasion we may be mistaken as to the source from which a particular and striking event has originated. But this is the exception rather than the rule, for in most instances the identifying marks between the works of God and the works of the Devil are quite apparent.

Since the days of the apostles the mountainous pile of historical evidence for answered prayer serves to support our faith in several ways. First, it confirms our confidence that what Scripture promises it actually fulfills. Second, it encourages us to try prayer for ourselves and to do so with faith and expectancy. But it also presses us to develop a spirit of boldness that laughs at apparent impossibilities and is not overtaken by surprise when the humanly unexpected and unanticipated comes to pass.

From the multiplicity of evidence we need only extract a few random samples to prove our point. Then our hearts will be encouraged, and we will take more seriously the privilege of prayer. We will begin to cultivate and develop the prayer life more seriously, and will grow in grace and in the knowledge of God.

George Whitefield was one of the world's truly great evangelists. He lived in a period of spiritual revival. In America this phenomenon was known as the Great Awakening. But it was not limited to America; it was felt around the world and especially in England. Associated in the movement were men like Jonathan Edwards, John and Charles Wesley, Gilbert Tennent, and Samuel Davies. But among all of them none shines more brightly than Whitefield and none was more successful and more mightily used of God. A few extracts from a biography will tell of answered prayer in his life and ministry.

Whitefield was in Savannah, Georgia, on this occasion. He had established an orphanage there. His biographer quotes him:

"And when we came to public worship, young and old—all —were dissolved in tears. After service several of my parishioners, and the little children returned home crying along the streets, and some could not avoid praying very loud." Being very weak he (Whitefield) lay down, but was soon roused by their cries and prayers and went to praying again. After they had prayed over an hour he desired them to retire, but they prayed on earnestly. A storm arose, and the loud peals of thunder and the lightning's vivid flash added much to the solemnity of the scene, that it reminded him of the Day of Judgment. Several of the orphans were very deeply impressed, and five hopefully converted. This was followed by a general awakening.[1]

In October of 1740 Whitefield, his biographer says,

reached New York . . . and preached in Mr. Pemberton's church the next evening with unusual power. Says he, "I never saw the Word of God fall with such weight in New York before. . . ." Although he had prayed earnestly for New York, yet feeling "somewhat dejected" as he approached it, "he expected but little movings there." But encouraged by his present prospects and past success there, he went forth and preached with such great power the next day that he felt "that a set time to favor New York was come." [2]

Whitefield often preached outdoors and in unlikely places. Not infrequently he set up a pulpit at race tracks and carnivals. His person and life were threatened and more than once only prayer delivered him from physical assaults. In one instance at Moorsfield in England he was under attack by several thousand ruffians.

"God's people kept praying. . . . A large body, quite on the opposite side, assembled together, and having got a large pole for their standard, advanced toward me with steady and formidable steps, till they came very near the skirts of our praying, and almost undaunted congregation. I saw, gave warning, and prayed to the Captain of our salvation, for present support and deliverance. He heard and answered; for just as they approached us with looks full of resentment, I know not by what accident, they quarreled among themselves, threw down their staff and went their way, leaving, however, many of their company behind, who before we had done, I trust were brought over to join the besieged party. I think I continued in praying, preaching and singing (for the noise was too great at times to preach), about three hours. We then retired to the tabernacle, with my pockets full of notes from persons brought under concern, and read them amidst the praise and spiritual acclamations of thousands, who joined with the holy angels in rejoicing that so many sinners were snatched in such an unexpected way out of the jaws of the devil." [3]

In May of 1742, accompanied by his wife, Whitefield sailed for Edinburgh. His own statement of what he did aboard ship and what transpired in Edinburgh illustrates how remarkable his prayer life was and how abundantly God responded to his petitions.

"On board," he says, "I spent most of my time in secret prayer. Satan shot many of his fiery darts against me, but with the shield of faith I was enabled to repel them all. As soon as I came on board the Holy Spirit filled my soul." . . . And when he came to Edinburgh, he says, "It would have melted you down to have seen them weep for joy. . . ." Encouraged by the good news, he says, "The work of God is beyond expression. . . . A minister tells me that scarce one is fallen back who was awakened, either among old or young." [4]

If we look for the secret that explains the unique accomplishments of Whitefield and accounts for the position he occupies in the annals of evangelism, it isn't hard to find and it is hardly a secret. Whitefield himself, perhaps without knowing it, laid bare the true explanation why God was able to use him so largely.

Thirsting for souls, he often preached to crowded houses before day and sung and prayed all night. "Whole days and weeks," he says, "have I spent lying prostrate on the ground in silent or vocal prayer." Striving to understand the Scriptures he read through Henry's Commentary on the Bible, on his knees, praying over every line of divine truth. . . . Prayer and his earnest devotional spirit, was the great secret of his success. [5]

Charles Haddon Spurgeon was a prince among English preachers. His prayer life was dynamic and daring. It explains in large measure his usefulness as a servant of God. It would be fair to say that had he been prayerless he would never have reached the heights that he did, nor would he have preached to thousands of people every Sunday, nor would he have seen the large number of conversions that resulted from his preaching.

Russell H. Conwell, of *Acres of Diamonds* fame, wrote a biography of Spurgeon. In it he enumerated many instances of answered prayer. Spurgeon, he said,

had been praying one night that the Lord would send gifts with which to supply the necessities of the Orphanage and a stranger in London was at the same time walking its foggy streets. He had never seen Mr. Spurgeon nor read any of his sermons, but he had heard his name mentioned. The impression upon that stranger's mind that same night was so great as to cause him to visit Mr. Spurgeon and make him a gift toward his church work. He had found it impossible to break away from the fascinating call. He rang Mr. Spurgeon's door-bell and insisted upon seeing Mr. Spurgeon and giving him a large sum of money. He refused at that time even to leave his name with Mr. Spurgeon, simply saying that he "lived many miles away." Afterward he sent another princely gift saying that the pleasure he had received from the other donation had made it one of the best investments of his life.[6]

When the great Tabernacle was begun Mr. Spurgeon prayed . . . that no workman might be injured during its construction. The prayer was so distinctly answered there that in the construction of a large business house near Ludgate Circus he was especially requested by the owners to come and offer the same prayer in connection with their enterprise. There were many old buildings to be pulled down and some very large ones to be constructed, yet in this case, as in the former, no persons were injured and the buildings were completed, to use the owners' expression, "with songs of grateful joy." [7]

These cases where his prayer was offered in one place and answered by some mysterious impression being made upon minds in another place with whom there was no natural means of communication were multiplied into the thousands. The history of all the great revivals at the Tabernacle presented numerous illustrations of this fact. Mr. Spurgeon prayed, and while he was praying or immediately thereafter, some person at a distance, felt it his duty to serve God in just the way, or by giving just the amount for which Mr. Spurgeon had asked." [8]

A remarkable case was mentioned in 1887 when Mr. Spurgeon at the request of friends made a special prayer in public for the conversion of a son and husband who were absent in

Australia. The friends who mentioned the matter to Mr. Spurgeon were new acquaintances to him, had but a few days before moved to London. They had never by word or by letter mentioned Mr. Spurgeon or his work to their friend in Australia. He now declares that he has never read anything of Mr. Spurgeon and does not remember that he had ever heard his name mentioned, although it was barely possible that he might have seen the name in some of the newspapers. But on the very day and at the very hour when Mr. Spurgeon engaged in a most fervent prayer, this man was at work upon a building in Melbourne. He stopped while carrying a timber from one portion of the building to another and said he was unable to go further, so quickly and so deeply was he impressed with a sense of his responsibility to God and of his lost condition of soul. He had not attended church during his stay in Australia, and was not a regular attendant at any church or chapel before he left England. The tears came to his eyes, his hands trembled, and he felt that he was forsaken of God because he had led such an unrighteous life. He was in no sense a criminal or immoral man, but this religious impression was so deep upon him that he went to the lowest story of the building, notified the superintendent that he must go to his boarding house. He went there and fell upon his knees and prayed for God's forgiveness and there received, as he afterwards testified, the "Light of Grace which reconciled him with his God." That same night before going to bed he wrote home to his people in London, telling them how he had, without the advice or guidance of any human being, been led to seek the Christ.[9]

Mr. Spurgeon's own son was converted in the same way, in direct answer to his (Spurgeon's) prayers when away from home. Mr. Drysdale felt it to be his duty to show the young man the way of righteousness and that impression to speak for Christ came to him with singular directness at the very hour when Mr. Spurgeon was praying the Lord that his son might be redeemed.[10]

The life story of J. Hudson Taylor, founder of the China Inland Mission (now the Overseas Missionary Fellowship), is one of continual answers to persevering prayer. Taylor was converted while his mother was on her knees away from home praying for that very thing to take place. Taylor himself was called of God to go to China with the good news of the Gospel. He resolved that he would have to learn to trust God alone for the supply of his material needs. In their book *Hudson Taylor's Spiritual Secret,* Dr. and Mrs. Howard Taylor spell out the details. Hudson Taylor determined

"To move man, through God, by prayer alone"—it was a great ambition, gloriously realized that lonely winter at Drainside.

"At Hull my kind employer (he continued) wished me to remind him whenever my salary became due. This I determined not to do directly, but to ask that God would bring the fact to his recollection, and thus encourage me by answering prayer.

"At one time as the day drew near for the payment of a quarter's salary, I was as usual much in prayer about it. The time arrived but Dr. Hardey made no allusion to the matter. I continued praying. Days passed and he did not remember, until at length on settling my weekly accounts one Saturday night, I found myself possessed of only one remaining coin— a half-crown piece. Still, I had hitherto known no lack, and I continued praying.

"That Sunday was a very happy one. . . . After concluding my last service about ten o'clock that night, a poor man asked me to go and pray with his wife, saying that she was dying. I readily agreed. . . ."

The man who asked Taylor to visit his wife was an Irishman who had requested a priest to come but the priest demanded eighteen pence payment which the Irishman did not have because his family was starving. Taylor arrived at the humble home and began praying but felt like a hypocrite because he had a half-crown in his pocket and did not wish to share it or part with it since it was

all that he had. Yet this family was in desperate straits. Taylor
wrote,

"Such a time of conflict came upon me as I had never
experienced before. How I got through that form of prayer I
know not, and whether the words uttered were connected or
disconnected. But I arose from my knees in great distress of
mind.

"The poor father turned to me and said, 'You see what a
terrible state we are in, sir. If you can help us, for God's sake
do!'

"At that moment the word flashed into my mind, 'Give to
him that asketh of thee.' And in the word of the King there is
power.

"I put my hand into my pocket and slowly drawing out the
half-crown gave it to the man, telling him it might seem a
small matter for me to relieve them, seeing that I was com-
paratively well off, but that in parting with that coin I was
giving him my all; but that what I had been telling them was
indeed true, God really was a Father and might be
trusted. . . .

"Not only was the poor woman's life saved, but my life as I
fully realized had been saved too. It might have been a wreck
—would have been, probably, as a Christian life—had not
grace at that time conquered, and the striving of God's Spirit
been obeyed.

"Next morning . . . the postman's knock was heard at the
door. . . . I looked at the letter, but could not make out the
handwriting. It was either a strange hand or a feigned one,
and the postmark was blurred. Where it came from I could
not tell. On opening the envelope I found nothing written
within, but inside a sheet of blank paper was folded a pair of
kid gloves from which, as I opened them in astonishment,
half-a-sovereign fell to the ground.

"Praise the Lord," I exclaimed, "four hundred per cent for
a twelve hours' investment. . . ." Then and there I determined that a bank that could not break should have my

savings or earnings as the case might be, a determination I have not yet learned to regret."

The half-a-sovereign was spent quickly. But Taylor's prayer for his employer to pay his salary remained unanswered. Two weeks went by. On a Saturday night Taylor's room rent was due to be paid. He prayed for the money. Dr. Hardey remembered that he owed Taylor money and when he mentioned it Taylor thought his prayers had been answered. But Dr. Hardey had no money that Saturday. He had put it all in the bank and it was Saturday night and none was forthcoming. Dr. Hardey left the surgery and behind him he left a perplexed and praying young man who sought the Lord for immediate help. Around ten o'clock Taylor prepared to leave the surgery to go home himself. The physician returned. One of his richest patients had come to his home to pay his bill. It had been much on the patient's heart and he felt he could not rest that Saturday night unless the bill was paid. Dr. Hardey had come to the surgery to write down the payment in the account book. He then turned to Hudson Taylor and gave him his money. His salary was paid! As his heart rejoiced Taylor later wrote:

"Again I was left, my feelings undiscovered, to go back to my little closet and praise the Lord with a joyful heart that after all I might go to China." [11]

Henry Clay Trumbull of the *Sunday School Times,* and a rare man of God, was also a man of prayer. In his biography of Trumbull, Philip Howard speaks of his prayer-power, and of the answers that came as a result of prayer. One in particular is striking, not because it has to do with spiritual matters but with mundane things that might be thought of as having little consequence. Howard says:

Henry Trumbull believed in prayer with a belief that kept nothing in reserve. It was always a characteristic glory of his nature that he trusted a friend freely and without question. When he had his Saviour's word for it on any subject, that was enough for him. He could trust that Friend above all others, and he did.

This was true in his Morgan Street work as elsewhere. In 1854 a Christmas party for the school had been under consideration. Something better than sliding bare feet on frozen pools—a neighborhood (sport)—was thought desirable. The day was close at hand, and the sleigh-ride which had been planned as the chief feature of the day's enjoyment was apparently not to be; for the weather was moderate, there was no snow or sign of snow, and to all appearance a fair spell had set in.

But all this was the Lord's work, reasoned the superintendent, and he could trust Him. So he advised all to go on with the plans for the sleigh-ride, and he prayed for snow. During the night before the appointed day the ground was covered to a sufficient depth with a snowfall that lasted just long enough for the ride.

That experience was never forgotten by the superintendent, or sophistically set aside as an accident. He knew no accidents. The Saviour was his Friend. Was that not enough? [12]

Norman Grubb of missionary fame writes of a tremendous prayer victory experienced by several missionaries under the Worldwide Evangelistic Crusade founded by the well-known cricketeer, C. T. Studd. Jack, Lily and Ivy Roberts, missionaries in Africa, were burdened for revival among their people. They

went to their own room terribly burdened. Throwing themselves on their faces before God, they spent the rest of the day alone in prayer. The next three days were given to secret intercession, and there grew a calm confidence that something out of the ordinary would happen when the conference opened. It began rather oppressively. Roberts preached on, "God commandeth all men everywhere to repent." But before he had finished the atmosphere changed. Obviously the Holy Spirit was working. At the noon meeting he spoke again from the same text. It was five o'clock before he stopped. At the close he said quietly, "Will those of you who want to get right with God do so now? The meeting is open for public confession of sin."

Confessions began with some of the leading Christians—their lack of love for God's Word and prayer, their slackness in giving. Then came a real break. One after another stood up and confessed to stealing. . . .

Then revival came. It was glorious and deep. Lives were transformed and the church renewed. Grubb says,

"The news (of the revival) went round, so that many were afraid to come and afraid of being mentioned in prayer. Some of the most notorious sinners of the district began to tremble. The news of prayer and answers to prayer came to be the common property of the tribe, even among the pagans." [13]

George Müller of Bristol is widely known for his orphanage ministry. Over a period of many years these orphans were supported by his prayers without asking men for money. Müller testified over and over again to thousands of answers to prayer that he received. One word he spoke reveals still another aspect of prayer and its answers that should encourage every heart that waits for answers that have not yet come. Müller said:

"I myself have for twenty-nine years been waiting for any answer to prayer concerning a certain spiritual blessing. Day by day I have been enabled to continue in prayer for this blessing. At home and abroad, in this country and in foreign lands, in health and in sickness, however much occupied, I have been enabled, day by day, by God's help, to bring this matter before Him; and still I have not the full answer yet. Nevertheless I look for it. I expect it confidently. The very fact that day after day, and year after year, for twenty-nine years, the Lord has enabled me to continue, patiently, believingly, to wait on Him for the blessing, still further encourages me to wait on; and so fully am I assured that God hears me about this matter, that I have often been enabled to praise Him beforehand for the full answer, which I shall ultimately receive to my prayers on this subject. Thus, you see, dear reader, that while I have hundreds, yea, thousands of answers, year by year, I have also, like yourself and others, the trial of faith concerning certain matters." [14]

William Carey is known as the father of modern missions. Beset by insuperable obstacles not the least of which was a wife who was mentally unbalanced, he translated the Word of God into many tongues and dialects and prepared grammars and dictionaries for various groups. Once he lost valuable manuscripts in a fire and was forced to repeat his labors. Nothing daunted this fearless follower of the cross. He, like so many of God's mighty warriors, was a man of prayer. His son, S. Pearce Carey, records how his father had a secret place where he talked with God. But infinitely more touching is the answer to prayer in the conversion of his son Jabez. Pearce wrote of his father:

> But Carey's sweetest comfort was the conversion of Jabez, for which he had long cried to God, and had entreated the prayers of such as Fuller and Ryland. The lad was filial, but not Christian. . . . Ryland . . . spoke of Carey's joy in Felix and William: "but he had a third son," he said, "giving him pain; because, though dutiful, he is unconverted." Pausing, he asked their instant prayers for Jabez, and a deep quiet fell on all, and they knew God was near and was hearing. Indeed, before they had called, God had answered. The very next Indian mail brought them the news that in the summer of 1812 Jabez had received into his contrite spirit Jesus as Saviour and as Lord. [15]

Rowland V. Bingham founded the Sudan Interior Mission. His long life and honored ministry was crowned by a prayer life that eventuated in the establishment of a missionary agency that today numbers some thirteen hundred workers. But not only did Bingham himself pray; he was prayed over, and numberless members of his mission have felt the touch of God in response to prayer.

In Bingham's early years he was sick unto death. Writing of that episode in his life at a later time he said: "Bishop Hill had called on me in the hospital in Lagos when my case was pronounced hopeless. On the afternoon when the doctor had written a note to my companions informing them that I could not live through the night, he had knelt at my bedside. When he returned to the Mission Home he gathered all the missionaries together and had special prayer on my behalf. As they rose from their knees, he turned to Miss Maxwell, the other survivor and said, 'Miss Maxwell, do you believe that we are going to receive that for which we have asked?' And he continued, 'I do. I believe that young man is going to be raised up.' He had prayed for me the real 'prayer of faith.' " And Bingham *was* raised up to continue his labors and establish that great mission.

In response to Bingham's own prayers the Sudan Interior Mission grew and waxed strong. The Canadian Keswick Conference was founded through his prayers. For twenty-five years Bingham edited the *Evangelical Christian* and he did it through prayer. One account written by Bingham himself will demonstrate his confidence in prayer. "Occasionally in our Council meetings we would record some little experience of direct answer to prayer at the home end. We remember one month especially when we had nothing with which to pay our rent as we did, in advance. We had heart-searching and much prayer, but the answer did not come until the close of the month. Then came a letter from a business man in New York saying that he had received a letter from a missionary in China whose business matters he looked after at the home end, instructing him to send us the exact amount we were needing for our rent. In closing his letter he said that he regretted having had his letter more than a month without attending to it. In speaking of the matter before the Council, we said we did not understand all the providences, but we did appreciate the fact that the Lord had moved the heart of His servant in far-away China in ample time for the supplying of our needs. One of the members of the Council, a man who was really wealthy, remarked: 'I am sorry that the Lord had to tell a poor missionary in China to do a thing that I might so easily have done at home.' Then he said, 'Mr. Bingham, if you are ever in need in that way again I hope you will come to me and let me know.'

"We remember the only time when we actually came to the end

of everything—even bread—these words of our wealthy friend recurred to us. Under the pressure of the home scene, with a wife who had stood with me to the limit and a little baby in the high-chair, I thought I would go and at least make a call on that brother. I met him at his home. I did not tell him that I had come to ask for bread. I tried to let him know that we were passing through difficult times, but I walked away no richer than I had gone, and with the secret determination that in the future I would turn my eyes upward rather than outward. The brother to whom we refer was one of the best men that ever lived. He was a splendid giver, and we have no reflection to make. We had early to learn to leave each of these brethren to their own stewardship, and to turn from judging them to the judging of ourselves. That very day we threw ourselves helpless and in desperation upon our Lord. He did a sweet thing. When we went to Him and asked for bread He did not give us a stone.

"Our landlord, who lived next door to us, was a grocer. He was one of the kindest of friends, and in those days when refrigerators were not common in the houses of people, he very kindly invited us to put our milk and butter in the grocery refrigerator. When we had finished up our bread that day my wife went to put the milk and butter left in the refrigerator. The grocer greeted her in his usual pleasant way and then remarked, 'Mrs. Bingham, the baker was in this morning, and he left some samples of rye bread. Take a loaf in and sample it and let me know what you think.' She brought the loaf in and we thought that rye bread tasted all right. It had something with it that day that I don't think rye bread ever had since.

"Lest our friends might think that our Heavenly Father is a poor provider I want to record the fact that this was the one solitary time in forty years when we were reduced to such straits. During forty years we can say that He has spread before us a bountiful table, and we think we have had as many of the natural pleasures and enjoyments as most lives can record. It was just these tests that gave us to know that every bit of the goodness and mercy of life are from His hand, and we have in consequence enjoyed them to the full. We would say, too, that through the years our Heavenly

Father knows not only how to provide an abundance, but also how to make a little go a long way." [16]

From the biography of Bingham there is another story of answered prayer surrounding the life of Tommie Titcombe, a close associate of Bingham's who although small of body was a great missionary and prayer warrior. Tommie Titcombe "relates a contact he had with the pagans and the Muslims that is strongly reminiscent of Elijah's contention with the Prophets of Baal. There had been no rain in the land for a long time. The crops withered, the fodder failed and starvation threatened. The pagans beat their drums, blew their horns, screamed and shouted to their idol. Pandemonium reigned for a week and the missionaries got little sleep. At the end of the week the pagans sacrificed a calf. They put blood upon the idol and drank the rest warm. Then they ate the animal raw. They didn't cook it. They were going to bring rain. But there was no rain. Let the missionary tell the rest of the story:

> I said, "Diaki, where is the rain?"
>
> He said, "White man, if you had not been here we would have sacrificed a girl. Our god always demands a human sacrifice. Then there would have been rain!" But there was no rain.
>
> The Muslims said, "We will bring the rain." If noise could have done it they would have brought the heavens down too. They screamed night and day. They cried to Mohamet, prayed three times a day and three times each night. They would not partake of a drop of water or morsel of food in the daytime. They were going to fast. They were going to bring the rain. They sacrificed a lamb, but there was no rain. So the week ended. The following day we were in church. I had just given my message when the African pastor came to me and said, "White man, isn't it time for us to pray for rain?"
>
> I said, "Listen, son, the pagans have been praying for rain for a week."
>
> "White man, we know that, but they are praying to idols that have eyes but they see not, ears that hear not and mouths that speak not. They cannot hear us. They can't help us."

"Well," I said, "what about the Muslims? They haven't any idols."

"White man, we know that Mohamet lived, but he died."

"What is the difference?" I said.

"Oh," he replied, "Jesus was born of a virgin, he lived and died."

"Is that all?"

"No, He came out of the grave and said, 'All power is given unto me in heaven and on earth.' "

"Have you any Scripture to give you assurance God will answer your prayer?"

He said, "Elias was a man of like passions as we are . . . and he prayed and the heaven gave rain."

I turned to the congregation and said, "Tomorrow night we are going to pray for rain. Let none come if they do not believe that God hears and answers prayer."

After the service I went to my little home. When the African pastor and I were sitting on the verandah, suddenly we heard the message of the drums. It was the bush telegraph telling all and sundry, "Now we shall see who has the God that lives—the believers are going to pray for rain."

So the message of the drums went forth into the gathering dusk of the golden African night, a challenge to the powers of darkness that held multitudes in the bondage of fear. That night we went to bed. Out of a cloudless sky, the silent stars looked down upon the parched earth, indifferent to the prayer of the pagan and Muslim alike beseeching their gods for the rain that would revive and refresh their dying world.

The next day was hot, so hot I warned my fellow-workers against going out into the sun. In the afternoon the heat was unbearable. At 7 P.M. the bell rang for church. There was not even a cloud the size of a man's hand to hang one's faith on. When I got to the church the Muslims were gathered on one side and the pagans on the other. There was an air of expectancy everywhere as though the prince of the power of the air knew that his authority was about to be challenged and his kingdom in that part of the earth assaulted.

When I entered the church I must confess I was surprised to see the Christians with big umbrella hats upon their heads.

"What are you doing with these things on your head in church?" I asked.

They looked at me with astonishment and reproach in their faces. "White man, haven't we come to pray for rain, and didn't you tell us that only those who believe God answers prayer were to come?"

Let me remind you that these were one-time cannibals, not far removed in years from those horrible rites. Many of them had eaten human flesh a few short years before—now they had come to pray for rain and, believing that the God who had saved them from their sins was the hearer and answerer of prayer, they had brought their umbrellas with them in full expectancy that their prayer for rain would be answered. My words were brief and confined to two verses from James 5, verses 17 and 18. Then they prayed. They did not pray for the white man, the pagans or the Muslims. Their prayer was simple, direct and went straight to the throne: "Lord we need rain." Ten minutes, fifteen minutes, twenty minutes went by as these black men with all the sublimity of their simple faith sought the help of God in their extremity. Then five minutes later there was a tapping on the corrugated iron roof of the church that thrilled us all, and in a moment the sound of abundance of rain. My, didn't it rain! The Lord just opened the windows of heaven so that the pagans and the Muslims fled in terror to their homes. The former cried: "We shouted for a week, and sacrificed a cow and got no rain"; the latter said, "We fasted for a week, and sacrificed a lamb, and we got no rain. But the Christians were only praying for a few minutes and God sent a deluge on the earth and has given us all the rain we needed. There is only one God and that is the God of the believers."

I had the joy of leading many of those pagans and Muslims to Jesus Christ, all because some simple people who had been brought out of the darkness of cannibalism by the power of the Lord Jesus Christ were willing to believe God's Word as

the Word of Him who cannot lie. Like Abraham of old they
staggered not at the promise of God through unbelief. They
sought God for rain as did Elijah, and God sent abundance of
rain. I have seen that done more than once, and many other
miracles in this realm of answered prayer." [17]

These illustrations of answered prayer make clear the claim of
Scripture that there is such a phenomenon as prayer, that God
hears the prayers of his people and that he provides answers to
their petitions. If this were not so the Bible would not be true. And
if the Bible is not true then men have no reliable guide to heaven
and no hope for help on earth. But the evidences for answered
prayer show that God's people have ample help on earth and this,
in turn, adds to their assurance that they also have a sure guide to
that life which lies beyond the grave.

This brings us full turn to the place at which we began this
pilgrimage. Prayer needs to be rescued from the fruitlessness which
has resulted from its universal neglect. The critical problem of our
day with regard to prayer is twofold: first it includes the ignorance
displayed by so many who claim Christ as Savior; and secondly
the undeniable fact that few people pray hard enough or take
prayer seriously enough to reap the maximum benefits that come
to those who use it rightly.

We do not claim too much when we say that the weakness of the
Church, the retreat from the Scriptures, the failure to see fruit
from evangelism, the slowdown of missionary outreach and enthu-
siasm, the apathy that has overtaken so many of the people of
God, and the general malaise that hangs over the body of Christ is
due in no small measure to prayerlessness. There is no reason to
believe that spiritual renewal and any great awakening will come
so long as this is true. Whenever the Church has gone forward, it
has done so on its knees. Until the Church returns to its knees and
takes up again the holy task of prayer there will be no large
advance of the kingdom and no strengthening of the churches.

For all who wish to see, the Scripture opens the door and holds
out the promise of blessing and renewal. When Solomon became
king of Israel he built the Temple. At its dedication the fire came

down from heaven. God appeared to Solomon in the night and spoke to him. He told him, "I have heard your prayer, and have chosen this place for myself as a house of sacrifice." Then God spoke to Solomon words that seem to be wholly out of context with respect to the dedication of the house, its acceptance by God and the promise of blessings that accompanied the building of the Temple. God foresaw the time when his people would be in a different frame of mind. He knew that sin and sloth would overtake them. Their first love would languish and instead of vitality and spiritual wholeness backsliding and deadness would characterize them. Therefore God spoke to Solomon: "If I shut up heaven that there be no rain, or if I command the locusts to devour the land, or if I send pestilence among my people, If my people, who are called by my name, shall humble themselves, and pray and seek my face, and turn from their wicked ways; *then* I will hear from heaven, and will forgive their sin, and will heal their land" (II Chron. 7:13,14).

It happened in Israel and it has happened in this hour—deadness, sloth, and spiritual anemia have come to us. Heaven has been shut up so that the earth is filled with evil and men walk in a thousand darknesses. Spiritual locusts have filled the land and the pestilence of racial hatred, sexual looseness, ethical relativity, spiritual flabbiness and Laodicean lukewarmness have diseased the Church. It is a sickness to death if the available remedy is not used. Humility, prayer, and turning from wickedness is the divine remedy that will restore the blessing, heal the land and cause our sins to be forgiven. More things have been wrought by prayer than this world dreams of. Why don't we try it?

Notes

[1] A. S. Billingsley, *Life of George Whitefield* (New York, 1891), p. 159.
[2] *Ibid.*, p. 181.
[3] *Ibid.*, pp. 220 ff.
[4] *Ibid.*, p. 224.
[5] *Ibid.*, p. 377.
[6] Russell H. Conwell, *Life of Charles Haddon Spurgeon*, 1892, p. 353.
[7] *Ibid.*, p. 353 f.
[8] *Ibid.*, p. 354.
[9] *Ibid.*, p. 357 f.

[10] *Ibid.*, p. 364.

[11] Dr. and Mrs. Howard Taylor, *Hudson Taylor's Spiritual Secret* (London: 1935), pp. 24 ff.

[12] Philip E. Howard, *The Life Story of Henry Clay Trumbull* (Philadelphia: 1905), p. 118.

[13] Norman P. Grubb, *With C. T. Studd in Congo Forests* (Grand Rapids: 1946), pp. 197 ff.

[14] Arthur T. Pierson, *George Müller of Bristol* (New York: 1944), p. 452.

[15] S. Pearce Carey, *William Carey* (Philadelphia: 1923), p. 299.

[16] J. H. Hunter. *A Flame of Fire* (Canada: 1961), pp. 73 ff.

[17] *Ibid.*, pp. 153 ff.